PRESENTED TO

....

FROM

....

DATE

....

it's still Possible

100 Reminders That God Can Do All Things

KAREN MOORE

THOMAS NELSON
Since 1798

Published in Nashville, Tennessee, by Thomas Nelson. Thomas Nelson is a registered trademark of HarperCollins Christian Publishing, Inc.

Published in association with the literary agency of Literary Management Group, LLC.

ISBN 978-1-4002-2235-3
ISBN 978-1-4002-2234-6 (audiobook)
ISBN 978-1-4002-2236-0 (eBook)

Printed in China

20 21 22 23 24 DSC 10 9 8 7 6 5 4 3 2 1

This book is dedicated to you, my beloved readers. It's yours to embrace when the future feels uncertain, or you face overwhelming odds, because God has given you a spirit of strength to overcome obstacles and fear. I believe you and God are always a force to be reckoned with and together you will find all that is still possible.

Introduction

"With men it is impossible, but not with God;
for with God all things are possible."
MARK 10:27 NKJV

You've been there. You've been to the place where you were ready to reach for a star, set your dreams in motion, get your life moving on the path you were certain it should go—and then the unexpected happened. Clouds became so thick you could hardly see your star, your dreams went off-kilter, and your path was constrained, severely limited, beyond difficult. You looked at it all and declared in your heart, "This is impossible!"

As a believer, you acknowledge the words of Jesus, reminding you that some tasks might not be possible for you, but they are possible for God. You know intellectually this is true, but how can those words bring comfort to your heart and mind when everything you hope for falls apart? How can you trust that God is guiding you past the obstacles and toward your goal?

The first step is to surrender your dreams, your hopes, and your very life to God, trusting that He is your guide and your infinite voice of possibility. Seek His face, knowing that on your own you can do nothing. Like David going out to slay the giant, Goliath, you must be ready to face the future undaunted, trusting that with God on your side, you can do anything.

These devotional readings will remind you of all that's possible, holding up the light so you can move forward and encouraging you to trust your Creator for everything you need. Get ready to put your life, your work, and what means the most to you into God's powerful hands. You can watch Him mold you and shape you within His world of possibility. It's your time to do impossible things.

Believing with you in all that is still possible,
KAREN MOORE

1

What Do You Believe?

Jesus looked at them intently and said, "Humanly speaking, it is impossible. But not with God. Everything is possible with God."

MARK 10:27 NLT

In the following scene from his book *Through the Looking-Glass*, Lewis Carroll shines a light on one of the biggest issues in the human experience:

> Alice laughed: "There's no use trying," she said; "one can't believe impossible things."
>
> "I daresay you haven't had much practice," said the Queen. "When I was younger, I always did it for half an hour a day. Why, sometimes I've believed as many as six impossible things before breakfast."

Alice is like most of us. She sees the reality of the world and cannot grasp how some things are even possible. Her mind is finite, and as she observes the world, she tosses the miraculous aside and quickly declares, "It's impossible!"

Perhaps the Queen in this tale believes as God would have us believe. She admits that she may not practice it enough, now that she's older, but somewhere in her younger days, she was able to believe many impossible things before breakfast.

Maybe it would help us if we would return to a more childlike faith, to the times when we believed in all that God can do—without question. Perhaps with a rekindled belief in all that is truly possible, we could focus on what brings us more assurance and more awareness of all God does.

When you are experiencing the bleak moments of life that cause your spirit to sag and your belief to waver, call out to the One who makes all things possible. After all, your life is in His hands, and He has unlimited power for good, for *your* good. He wants to carry you through each dark moment into His glorious light. Why? Because He knows all that is possible and He wants you to know it too.

So ask yourself: What *do* you believe?

Lord God, I often believe I have no choices or no possibilities for success in the situations I face. Rekindle my unwavering belief in You, and remind me to put my life in Your hands every day. I trust You will guide me toward those things that are meant for me. Help me to fully believe You are God of all that is possible! Amen.

2

Impossible Faith

Then Jesus said to the centurion, "Go your way; and
as you have believed, so let it be done for you."

MATTHEW 8:13 NKJV

The centurion had a faith most of us can admire. He knew his
servant was in a life-threatening situation. Local physicians
couldn't heal the man, so he did the one thing that could make a
difference. He went straight to Jesus.

As the centurion, an officer of the Roman army, put his
request before Jesus, he also did two important things. First, he
told Jesus that he was a man who commanded authority. When
he ordered others to come or go, they did so. But despite his power
and prestige, the centurion felt unworthy for Jesus to come to his
home. Second, the centurion believed in Jesus' power to heal,
and he trusted in Him completely. He believed that Jesus could
perform the impossible. Jesus only had to say the word and his
servant would be healed.

Jesus marveled at the man's faith. He marveled because this
centurion was used to being in charge, the one who was served
by others, yet he humbled himself before Jesus on behalf of his

servant. He didn't try to rely on his own strength or order Jesus to do what he wanted. Instead, he surrendered his ego and his heart and believed in what Jesus could do. He also petitioned Jesus for the sake of his servant, not for himself or for a son or father, but for his servant.

Does your belief system support you and bolster your faith? Do you trust that simply believing in Christ with your whole heart and surrendering your title, your position in the world, or your sense of self-worth will make a difference?

That is what God is asking you to do. He wants you to trust Him with your life, with every person you love, and with all the strength you possess, leaving everything to Him. He is asking you to have an impossible faith.

God of All That's Possible, help me to believe deeply, fully, and unconditionally in what You can do. Bless me with an impossible faith to trust You regardless of the circumstances. I surrender my will and all that I am to Your care and keeping. I trust in You for all that I am yet to be. Amen.

3

Beyond What You See

"See, I am doing a new thing! Now it springs up;
do you not perceive it? I am making a way in the
wilderness and streams in the wasteland."

ISAIAH 43:19

Life is complicated and sometimes perplexing. Hymn writer Frances Ridley Havergal wrote, "In perplexities, when we cannot tell what to do, when we cannot understand what is going on around us, let us be calmed and steadied and made patient by the thought that what is hidden from us is not hidden from Him."

Most of us wish we could see around corners, or at least to the end of whatever crisis we're facing. We want to know the outcome, get over the issues, and move on. In the midst of our troubles, we sometimes imagine that even our prayers are not sufficient to deal with our problems.

Perhaps you've resigned yourself to minimal effort because the thing you're facing is simply not fixable. The problem is beyond your control, and you tell yourself it's probably too big for God to handle as well. You imagine all is lost and your short-sighted faith only increases your misery.

Havergal reminds us that nothing is hidden from God and nothing surprises the Creator of the universe, the One who remains ever faithful and omniscient. If you believe that in God is endless possibility, that He can make a way through the wilderness of your life and open up springs of living water when you're lost, then you have the ability to let Jesus fill you with calm. You can move from a place of needing to see what lies ahead to a place of prayerfully closing your eyes and resting in the knowledge that God is already doing His good work.

Let go of needing the answers and simply let God be God. He will help you see the path more clearly in His time because He goes ahead of you and knows every step you must take. Remember that He is the author of new things, the only One who can make streams in the deserts of our lives. What new thing would you have Him do for you today? Close your eyes and trust that God sees beyond what you see.

Lord, thank You for walking ahead of me to clear the path and open the doors to new possibility. Help me to trust so completely in You that I can close my eyes in prayer and peacefully rest in Your grace and mercy. Amen.

4

Think Big ... No, Bigger!

Think about the things that are good and worthy of praise.
Think about the things that are true and honorable
and right and pure and beautiful and respected.
PHILIPPIANS 4:8 NCV

t's not easy to put on a happy face when it feels as if nothing in your life is coming together. You've prayed and believed and acted in all the ways that make sense to you, but nothing has changed. You begin to wonder if God even knows about the mess you're in, the burdens you bear. Maybe God doesn't care or He's too busy with the rest of the world to bother with you and your troubles. Where does that leave you?

When you're going through a rough patch where everything in life feels upside down, you may be struggling to hold on to hope. When even your friends don't know how to comfort you, you might slip into negative thinking that tries to convince you that you're not on God's list of favorites. But you can change your thoughts!

If you want to step out of the doldrums and move forward into God's promises and peace, start by changing your heart and mind. Stop counting your miseries and start counting your blessings. That's a great place to start. You only need to shift your focus so you can see God's hand at work right now.

The writer of Philippians suggests that we open our minds to new possibilities by thinking new things; we can alter our perspective by thinking about big things—and even bigger things! Recall what you've experienced that made you feel joyful and aware of God's gracious hand at work, and then give God the praise.

Once you start counting your blessings, you'll have nowhere to go but up. Your face will feel the warmth of the sun, and your heart will be quickened by the knowledge that God is near. You will notice how your thought patterns change, shifting from negativity and disappointment to thankfulness and hope.

Change your thoughts today and reflect on all that brings you genuine joy. Look for God to show up *right now* and shine His face upon you, ready to make all things new. Keep thinking bigger and bigger—brighter and better—because you serve a great big God, and He makes all things possible!

Lord, I get caught up in the swirling frustrations and miseries noisily bombarding my mind, and I forget how to quiet them again. I know that all I really need is You and the gentle reminder that You have bigger plans for my life. Help me to meditate on the big things that are possible for an even bigger God. Amen.

5

He Makes All Things New

Because of the LORD's great love we are not consumed,
for his compassions never fail. They are new
every morning; great is your faithfulness.

LAMENTATIONS 3:22–23

C an you remember the last time you really felt excited about getting something new? Maybe as a kid you waited patiently for a new bike on your birthday. Maybe you just graduated, and life beckoned you to your first job or first apartment. It was amazing to have the whole world at your fingertips. The possibilities were endless! You were ready to create the adventure of a lifetime. What an exhilarating feeling! Do you remember?

By now, you've experienced more of life in all its fullness, embracing the ups with delight and weathering the downs with prayer and frustration and sadness. You may wonder whether you've missed the big adventure you once thought would happen. Maybe you feel that those days of innocent dreams have passed you by. What if the promise of a beautiful life simply isn't true?

But let's ask a different question: What if God has been saving some of the best adventures *for this moment in time*? What if, in His great love for you, He has faithfully and patiently waited for you to have enough life experience to be ready for what He has next?

The One who loves you and sees you right where you are makes things new for you every morning. He knows everything about you and wants you to remember what it's like to try something so new that it is a little bit scary. God doesn't care about your age. He doesn't assign limitations because you've blown out a few dozen birthday candles. He's still working with one incredible human whom He designed for greatness . . . you!

As you begin today, remember that God makes all things new, and there are still possibilities up ahead. Remember the delight of anticipation, embrace the joy of changing obstacles into opportunities, and turn your face toward heaven. Let God know that you believe in all His possibilities, greater things than you've ever known before simply because of who He is!

You may find yourself embracing a whole new you.

Lord, help me believe that You have a great plan for my life, that Your compassion and Your mercies are new every morning. Help me anticipate the possibilities of all that can happen as I follow You. Let me trust You and believe with my whole heart that You are not done with me yet. Make my heart and mind new in You today. Amen.

6

It's Not Too Late

To you, a thousand years is like the passing of
a day, or like a few hours in the night.

PSALM 90:4 NCV

Your smartphone holds time captive for you. Though you may not consciously consider the flickering hours, somewhere inside your mind is a very real sense that a clock is ticking, and your life is passing.

You may even worry that time will run out before you accomplish all the things you intend to do. You cringe when you mismanage your time. Maybe you once dreamed you'd be a ballet dancer or a rock star, but now you smile at your unfounded and ungrounded ambitions.

Though childhood fantasies may not pan out, other sweet possible dreams still linger. Those dreams urge you to trust it's not too late to accomplish great things. After all, God designed you to be a unique and special person, and He inspired your skills and talents. He also equipped you to accomplish all He created you to be.

So it's up to you. Will you give up your dreams, or will you look up and trust that God has more for you? Will you say it's too late for you, too late to accomplish those desires still burning in your heart? God sees past the limits you've already placed on yourself. You may never be in the spotlight at the ballet, but you can still be on your toes, kick up your heels, and take a leap of faith. You may not be a rock star, but you can sing God's praises to anyone with an ear to hear and a heart to receive His love.

You are right on time to execute God's plans and direction. God is so proud of all that you are and all you are yet to be. He knows that with His help, you are bound to do impossible things!

Father in heaven, thank You for the hours and minutes that make up my days. Help me to embrace life with great joy, trusting in You to guide me into being all that You designed me to be. Help me not to feel discouraged by how much time has passed and to believe that You will show me the way at the perfect time. I praise Your name, ready to make each day count according to Your plan and purpose. Amen.

7

I Will Teach You

"Now go! I will help you speak, and I will teach you what to say." But Moses said, "Please, Lord, send someone else."

EXODUS 4:12–13 NCV

You may recall that God's hand was on Moses' life from the very beginning. He had quite a divine start, saved from certain death at his birth when all Hebrew male babies were sentenced to die. Then his mother set her infant son adrift in a basket on the Nile River, and he was rescued by the pharaoh's daughter and raised as royalty. That kind of backstory should have filled Moses with confidence that God could do anything.

Scripture reminds us, however, that even though Moses was called by God and had conversations with Him and saw demonstrations of God's great power, Moses still had doubts about whether God knew what He was doing. Moses doubted he could do the job God wanted him to do. Even after God said, "I will teach you what to say," Moses replied, "Send someone else."

Moses' response might surprise you, but perhaps you have responded the same way. Maybe doubt gets in the way of tasks you are meant to accomplish, taking away your opportunities.

Have you told God to send someone else for the job He's called you to? Have you doubted that you have what it takes?

Moses was an older man when this conversation happened. He had spoken to God face-to-face and had experienced the impossible phenomenon of the burning bush, and yet Moses doubted God's calling on his life. He believed there had to be someone better for God to send instead.

What causes you to doubt God's plans and direction for your life? If you're hesitant to follow God's call because of fear and doubt, God may be telling you to trust Him. He never makes a mistake. He will give you all the tools and guidance you need for His plan to be successful.

If you want to embrace life in all its scariness *and* hopefulness, you have to get past your own fears and doubts. You have to stop saying, "Send someone else," and realize that God wants to send you. He signed on with you before you were born, and He's been watching over you ever since. He knows what you can do and what you have to learn, but He will teach you everything you need to know.

Let God know you're ready to serve Him in big ways. With God by your side, you can accomplish great, even impossible, feats.

Lord, I'm not always sure what it is that You would have me do, but I am ready to serve You in new ways and in big ways. Speak to my heart and remind me of all that You want me to be, and I will say, "Send me, Lord, send me!" Amen.

8

Remember Who You Are

You belong to Christ, so you are Abraham's
descendants. You will inherit all of God's blessings
because of the promise God made to Abraham.

GALATIANS 3:29 NCV

*C*urrent technology affords instant gratification when we're searching for answers. When we have questions, we can search the Internet and find helpful, though not necessarily correct, answers for our circumstances. Often the answers leave God out of the equation.

Sometimes we have questions about who we are and why we're here. Have you ever asked, "What's my purpose?" God knows us better than we can ever know ourselves. He promises to help us when we come to Him with our questions and concerns. When we're searching for answers, God wants to be the first One we turn to. When Google is long gone, God will still be the greatest source of power and understanding available. Today's key verse, God's promise to Abraham, still stands because God doesn't change. He is the same yesterday, today, and forever. So what does that mean for you?

Start by looking at who you are. You are a child of God. That means you are supported by His eternal promises. He walks with you and shares in your hopes and dreams. He sees your frustrations and your challenges and is prepared to offer guidance and peace. He knows exactly who you are created to be.

You have a rich resource that you can tap into at any time. When you trust in who you are as God's child, your dreams take on greater dimension and opportunity for fulfillment. You are strengthened by God's promises that He will draw near to you and always love you.

If you're struggling with who you are and what you should be doing with your life, you may find the Internet can supply you with some leads, but only God can supply all your needs. Only God knows who you truly are and the kind of person you have the potential to become. Seek His face and remember who you are, a blessed child of God.

Lord, thank You for reminding me to trust in Your promises, and help me to remember that You will always be here for me, no matter what I face. Thank You for Your steadfast love and faithfulness. Thank You for not only listening to my questions but also providing me with answers in Your perfect timing. Amen.

9

What Is an Abundant Life?

*"The thief comes only to steal and kill and destroy; I came
that they may have life, and have it abundantly."*
JOHN 10:10 NASB

f we did a survey to discover what people imagine to be a
life of abundance, we'd receive a variety of definitions. Some
would say it involves having more than enough money or owning
fancy cars. Others might think an abundant life means being rich
in experiences, having the ability to travel the world, or finding
fulfillment in everyday life.

God wants you to have an abundant life, more than you might
dream possible. Ponder what an abundant life means to you. In
today's world, it's easy to be swept up in the idea that only mate-
rial possessions equal abundance and fulfillment. Sometimes the
thieves of anxiety and fear steal not only our belief in having an
abundant life but also our willingness to allow God to bless us
with abundance according to His will.

Jesus came so you could enjoy life in all its fullness. God
wants your heart to overflow with gladness because of what He
has done. If you allow God to work in your life, you may well

experience abundant joy, over-the-top possibility, enormous peace, and a sense of love and well-being like you've never known before. Jesus redeemed you so that you might have an abundant, filled-to-the-brim, beyond-belief life experience.

What does having an abundant life mean to you today? You might need to reassess your priorities. Think about what brings you heartfelt joy, unexpected pleasure, and closeness in your relationship with God. Notice how God has moved through your life, blessing you with abundance in so many ways.

Lord, I am in awe of all that You have done to allow me to live a happy, fulfilled, and authentic life. Even when life isn't going my way, I know I have all that I need because I have You. Help me to share Your blessings with people I meet today. Amen.

10

Be a Little Bit Daring

Cast your bread on the surface of the waters,
for you will find it after many days.
ECCLESIASTES 11:1 NASB

The British author and photographer Cecil Beaton once wrote, "Be daring, be different, be impractical, be anything that will assert integrity of purpose and imaginative vision against the play-it-safers, the creatures of the commonplace, the slaves of the ordinary."

A similar message can be read in Ecclesiastes 11:1, which says, "Cast your bread on the surface of the waters" and see what happens. Discovering all that is possible often means you must move past what you know and take a chance. You must be willing to be bold. Casting bread on the waters is an interesting metaphor. Literally, you would see little pieces of bread spreading out and floating away one by one. Some bread would become dinner for a passing fish, but some pieces, at least those that represent new opportunities, will go beyond your expectation where new possibilities emerge.

What bread can you cast on the waters? Is it your vision for a new product or service, your time or talents? Or perhaps it's your goals and intentions? Renewed faith, slowly moving beyond the bounds of your comfort zones and routines, guiding you with hope, has the ability to change your life. Nothing can happen, nothing can go forward, if you do not take the first step. Is God calling you to be a bit more daring, somewhat impractical, and step outside of your safety zone? Is He asking you to trust Him and take that next step?

Jesus came to earth and stepped into a world that wasn't fully prepared for Him. He cast His Spirit on those around Him with daring and with integrity of purpose. He knew who He was and what He had to offer. He never doubted God's plan, even when He could not see the fruit of His labors. He simply kept being the One who shared a different point of view and who went against the "play-it-safers" of His day.

One way you can share in His imaginative vision is to step out in faith, moving beyond what you know and choosing to believe God has a way to make things work together for good. Today is the perfect day to cast your bread upon the waters of faith and see what God has in mind for you.

Lord, I'm ready now to step forward in faith, opening myself up to new possibilities. Thank You for going before me and pushing me past the commonplace and the ordinary. Amen.

11

Knocked Down, but Not Out!

Now here I am, eighty-five years old. I am still as
strong today as I was the day Moses sent me out, and
I am just as ready to fight now as I was then.
JOSHUA 14:10–11 NCV

Some days everything feels like a challenge. You're stuck in a line of traffic as you desperately try to get to the airport. Your flight is canceled, and the next one is hours away. Your boss has no sympathy for your situation and expects you to work miracles. You're knocked down, but you're not out.

This passage from Joshua is a great reminder to those of us who find excuses for why we haven't moved forward or why we've given up the fight to accomplish what we know God has placed on our hearts. We might say we are too old, or too busy, or too out of shape to get back in the game, but it might be that the one key area of our lives that is out of shape is our attitudes.

Joshua lived to fight, not just because he was a scrapper but because he was a man on a mission. No matter how old he was or what his circumstances looked like, he had things to accomplish for God. He didn't make excuses.

You may feel you don't have any fight left in you. You're spent. You're overwhelmed with life and nothing about it seems easy. So what do you do? Perhaps you take a note from Joshua, and you show back up for your life. You prepare for the fight with all you've got. You don't do it for yourself because you already know that you can't fight any battle alone. You do it for God, letting Him know you are still here, still ready to do His will.

God is willing to give you the strength you need if you're willing to give Him the courage of your convictions. He will build you up, renew your spirit, and lead you to victory. Tell Him you're still willing and able to take up His cause. You may be down, but you're not out when God is on your side. Your willingness to move forward is all that's necessary for the God of What's Possible to guide you toward your heart's desires.

Lord, I often feel defeated, and in that state of mind I know I don't accomplish very much. I pray that You will strengthen and renew me in body, mind, and spirit so that I might stand up and fight for Your causes in this world. Amen.

12

Blessed to Be You

The LORD said to Abram, "Leave your country, your relatives,
and your father's family, and go to the land I will show you.
I will make you a great nation, and I will bless you."
GENESIS 12:1–2 NCV

When God changed Abram's name to Abraham, He had a big vision of what He wanted Abram to do. God knew Abraham would trust Him, and He knew He could count on Abraham. Abraham was considered righteous before God.

God's request of Abraham: leave your country and everything you know and go to a strange land. Imagine that. What if God told you to get up and move halfway across the world? In Abraham's case, if he was willing to obey, God would bless him beyond measure, make him famous, and let all the world know what a righteous man he was. God would bless Abraham in every way so he could bless others. Together they would build God's kingdom.

You may not have to leave your familiar place to do God's work in the world. You may be called to stay right where you are and help the people in your neighborhood. You may be blessed with skills and talents that bring fulfillment to others.

Your gifts are not to be underestimated. God designed you to stand apart in unique ways from those around you. No one can do exactly what you do the way you do it. You are blessed to be you. And the more you obey God's call on your life, the more blessings you will see and feel around you.

Thank God for the ways He has blessed your life, and do all you can to bless others with a renewed attitude. Open your heart and mind so you understand just how God is calling you to obey Him.

Lord, bless me with the courage to step out in faith as Abram did when You first called him. I want to do the best I can to bless those around me according to Your will and purpose. Thank You for blessing me as I learn to step up and step out in faith. Amen.

13

The God of Second Chances

GOD, my God, I yelled for help and you put me together.
GOD, you pulled me out of the grave, gave me another
chance at life when I was down-and-out.
PSALM 30:2–3 MSG

Most of us appreciate a second chance. We want another chance to make up with our spouse after a disagreement. We want to prove to the boss we can fix an issue we caused. We want to know time has not run out, leaving us with no options, no way to make amends for our mistakes.

The beauty of the psalm quoted here is that David is reminded of all the times God rescued him. He sees that God has literally rescued him from death and revived him when he was down-and-out. Without God's help, David knows he would not have survived.

Perhaps David knew that because God loves unconditionally, we are not only given second chances but third and fourth and infinite chances to do better. Because of God, you live in a world of infinite possibility. He still blesses you with opportunities to open new doors, plant new seeds, and fulfill the desires of your heart, because the God of second and third and fourth chances is the One in control. He sees you, and He knows when you need to be given more time, more instruction, and more energy to try again. He sustains your soul and stays by your side.

As you reflect on this truth, consider the people in your life. Are there any who need you to give them a second chance, to forgive them and make amends? God's gift of grace sustains you each day and allows you to correct your course and move on. You can offer that same grace to those around you. When you do, it will strengthen your connection to God. You become part of God's plan to make things new, to make forgiveness possible, and to open the doors to amazing possibilities.

Lord, I am grateful that You are so willing to give me second chances. I pray that I will be more aware of creating an atmosphere around me that allows others to try again when they fall down. Thank You for endless chances to make amends with Your steadfast love and forgiveness. Amen.

14

The Blind Spots

"Why do you notice the little piece of dust in your friend's eye,
but you don't notice the big piece of wood in your own eye?"

LUKE 6:41 NCV

If we're honest, we would admit we have blind spots—areas of life where we don't see clearly. We make snap judgments about someone else's behaviors but fail to recognize our own unwise choices. Jesus says we need to work on our own blind spots before we try to work on the flaws of others.

Take a look in the mirror. Perhaps you would be surprised to see you have gotten stuck in a rut or that you've stopped growing spiritually. Are there areas in your life where you can improve? Are there struggles in your heart that you need to bring to the light? Reflect on the steps you could take to improve your current situation.

We often lose sight of possibility because we put up roadblocks. We set up obstacles of fear or doubt. Have you ignored inspiration and the nudging from God's Spirit that He still has greater plans for your life? Have you settled into a more commonplace life, leaving the "big piece of wood in your own eye"?

Refusing to move forward and leaving your blind spots untouched dims your opportunities.

Today you're invited to think again about the dreams you once held dear and ask yourself the hard questions. *What is stopping me from going after my dream now? What obstacles have I put in my own way? What blind spots are keeping me from seeing God's will for my life?*

Ask Jesus to guide you into all possibility. Shift your focus from other people's flaws and shortcomings to your own so that Jesus can show you ways to improve and become more of who He created you to be. Surrender your doubts and fears and trust that with Him by your side, you can yet accomplish great things. You may be amazed at what you discover with your eyes and heart wide open. Let God's incredible Spirit light your way into greater possibilities.

Lord, I know that I have some major blind spots in my thinking, and I often make excuses for not moving forward. Help me heal the blind spots that keep me from seeing the amazing ways You are working in my life. Open my eyes and help me remember that with You by my side, my possibilities are endless. Amen.

15

God Gives You Victory

I put no trust in my bow, my sword does not
bring me victory; but you give us victory over our
enemies, you put our adversaries to shame.

PSALM 44:6–7

t may seem odd, but for some of us winning, accomplishing our goals, or becoming successful may be the very things that keep us from moving forward. Sometimes we start to believe success is our own doing. We feel independent of God, as though we might not need Him as much as we do during difficult times. This misplaced feeling of independence can hinder our spiritual growth and halt the deepening of our faith.

From the time King David was a boy, he knew the only way he could defeat his enemies was if he trusted God to go with him. He knew he could do nothing by himself. Throughout his lifetime he often was victorious over his foes, but he never imagined it was all his doing. He knew he couldn't face any enemy alone. God blessed him with victory.

When you have a season of success, it feels good. Life feels easy, and you often forget God has a hand in your victories. You think you've arrived at your successes based on your hard work and determination alone. So when a day of defeat happens, it isn't always easy to get back on your feet and try again. A loss might cause you to believe that the glory days are over. You might think you don't have the support or abilities you once had. Fear moves in and whispers that you cannot win. Setbacks don't mean it's impossible for you to reach victory again. You are forgetting one important truth: God is the One who gives you victory.

One thing the most successful winners know is that they aren't victorious all by themselves. They didn't reach the heights alone. Likewise, you are not alone either and you never will be. You are a child of God and so you have all the powers of heaven at your disposal. You have strength that goes beyond your imagination because with God all things are possible. The key is not to rely on your own strength. Don't believe that who you were in the past is who you are meant to be in the future. God is teaching you how to push through the losses so you can rise higher, soar greatly, and accomplish more for Him. Be blessed because you are meant to win again and again. God wants you to thrive and know that with Him, it's still possible to have hope in your dreams.

Lord, thank You for being with me even when I don't acknowledge Your presence. Thank You for loving me continually and helping me to become the person I am meant to be. With You, Lord, I know I can move toward victory. Amen.

16

Yes, You Get a Do-Over

"Amend your ways and your doings."
JEREMIAH 7:3 KJV

f you're a golfer, you may have had an opportunity to take a mulligan, a do-over, a chance to try again on that poor shot you just made. The beauty of the mulligan is that it isn't factored into your score. It's like you are taking the shot for the first time. Of course, when you get a mulligan, you want to do it right; you want to take your best shot.

In life we don't always get a chance to take a mulligan. If you can't make your credit card payment, you get dinged immediately with an extra charge. If you speak an unkind word to your friend, it may be held against you for years to come. You can't take it back. You don't get a do-over.

The Father of us all takes a different approach to our mistakes once we have accepted His Son into our hearts. He looks at us and says, "I have redeemed you, and My Son has paid the price for your mistake. Go on and try again. Do it over and do it better this time!" You get a holy mulligan.

Most of us make some error in judgment every day, but God

is not keeping score. Does He want you to do better by treating others with love and respect? Of course, He does! Because of the work of Jesus and because of your faith in Him, you get another chance. You get to do it better next time. But this also means that you should offer the same grace to others.

Remember that you live in grace and possibility because the God of your heart has redeemed you and paid the price for your mistakes. He has done it once and for all. What He wants in return is your honest effort to try to do better. God will bless every step you take.

Lord, thank You for giving me a chance to correct my course and walk more closely with You. Help me to do things right the first time, and give me grace when I need to try again. My heart longs to please You today. Amen.

17

You Are God's Love Letter

You yourselves are our letter, written on our
hearts, known and read by everyone.
2 CORINTHIANS 3:2 NCV

Think of the people you admire the most. Chances are they hold your respect and admiration because of the ways they act toward you and others. Perhaps they are strong leaders but have an ability to show compassion and kindness in the midst of giving direction. Perhaps you respect them because they aren't afraid to be themselves and they work hard to accomplish their dreams.

In his letter to the Corinthians, Paul reminds the people who they are. They are the examples of Christ. They are the love letters from God written to a world in need of all He has to offer. They are known for the kindnesses they show and the impact they have on the people around them. In other words, he wants them to remember that their actions matter. What they do makes a difference.

When you think of your life, keep in mind that you, too, are God's love letter. You are His example of grace and compassion and humility. You demonstrate what it means to be God's child to those in your midst. It is helpful to remember that your light is always on, and it reflects the deeper matters of your heart. You may lead others to Christ simply by being in their presence.

It's still possible that you will be the reason someone will spend eternity in heaven. You make that possible by knowing who you are in Christ. God makes it possible by putting others in your path who need to discover He is there for them.

If one of your dreams is to make a difference in the world, open your mind and heart to the idea that you can make a difference, not only in this world but also in the world to come. There's nothing sweeter than sharing a love letter. Tell others what God has done for you today. You may be their light of possibility.

Father in heaven, I pray that I will be an example of Your love and grace. I pray that You will strengthen my spirit and cause Your light to shine brightly. Be with me as I encounter others today, and let me demonstrate Your mercy and peace. Amen.

18

Cleaning Up the Cobwebs

Create in me a clean heart, O God, and
renew a steadfast spirit within me.
PSALM 51:10 NKJV

St. Augustine of Hippo once wrote this note to God: "The house of my soul is too small for you to come to it. May it be enlarged by you. It is in ruins: restore it."

Perhaps one of the best ways to receive all that God believes to be possible for our lives is for us to clean out the cobwebs of the past and make room for God in our hearts. After all, if we've got a pile of old memories that grieve our spirits, stomp on our efforts, and smudge our hopes, then it may be time to clean up.

You might actually suppress God's Spirit by holding on to old garbage, stuff covered in cobwebs, forgiven by God long ago. Even with His forgiveness, you may have left the old trunk of despair somewhere close as a reminder of what God has done in your life. It might feel impossible to completely let go of your past, but with God this is a task you can accomplish. Get out the broom and sweep out those old mistakes because He doesn't need you to hold on to those things. Your past only clutters up spaces in your heart and makes it hard for you to open your mind to what God has for you now.

Perhaps it helps to pray like St. Augustine and ask God to enlarge your heart and clean up those spaces that no longer serve you. Throw a few things out and make room for opportunities to be holier. If you need the Carpenter of your soul to do a major renovation, go ahead and ask. He'll be there for you. Have courage to open your heart and let light in. God wants more for you, and when you make room for Him, He can do wonders.

Imagine how good you'll feel when the work is done! All you have to keep in mind is that you have now let in the fresh air of God's Spirit and His gracious light so that He can make even more things possible in your life.

Lord of the Possible, thank You so much for taking that dead space where I store old sins and helping me clean it out. With the help of Jesus, I'm ready to rebuild my temple and make it a beautiful place for You to live. The door is open wide; please come on in. Amen.

19

Remembering Grandma Moses

Therefore we do not lose heart. Though outwardly we are
wasting away, yet inwardly we are being renewed day by day.
2 CORINTHIANS 4:16

Grandma Moses might not be a name you recognize. She was born in 1860 and died in 1961. When Grandma Moses was seventy-three years old, she started a new career. She decided she wanted to paint, and it turned out she was a phenomenal folk artist. In fact, in 2006 one of her paintings sold for nearly a million and a half dollars. It makes you wonder if somewhere within herself she said, "I'd like to make a living as an artist. I believe it's still possible!" Even if she didn't say that, she certainly acted on it. She didn't let her age cause her to lose heart or stand in the way of her desire to accomplish a new dream.

Since God placed a portion of His Spirit within us, you can be certain that no matter what your body is doing on the outside, your inner spirit, the one that causes you to persevere and try again, is still going strong. You are being renewed every day by the Spirit. Perhaps not physically but emotionally and spiritually. And that means you still have a future.

What difference could you make in the world if you tried something new? What would happen if you didn't make excuses for *why* you can't do what your heart is calling you to? What if you didn't let your age, your missed opportunities, your negative self-image get in the way of what you can still do? You may be amazed at what a willing spirit coupled with God's divine Spirit can do.

Grandma Moses is a wonderful example of what is possible regardless of age. Perhaps as a Christian, you can take that a step further. You can believe that you can do more by inviting God to walk along with you. It's a good way to ponder what you'd like to do next. Step out in faith, brush up on your painting, and try something new because the world awaits what you can do.

Father God, please help me not to lose heart. I am not clear about the path ahead of me. I might not know what special talents or hidden skills exist in me that I have never addressed, but I trust You know what I can do. Help me believe that I can do all things through Christ who strengthens me. Amen.

20

Stepping into New Shoes

*Yet the LORD says, "During the forty years that I
led you through the wilderness, your clothes did not
wear out, nor did the sandals on your feet."*

DEUTERONOMY 29:5

Most of us own more than one pair of shoes. In fact, most of us have a wide variety for various occasions. Having our shoes wear out is probably not something we worry about.

The people who walked with Moses couldn't stop by a shoe store. The fact is they didn't need to because their shoes never wore out. Not in forty years! One of the miracles they experienced was that God protected their clothes and shoes.

Can you even imagine wearing the same outfit for forty years and having it remain as fresh and new as the first day you put it on? That's a miracle! That's the work of God in the details, the work of the same God who watches over you day after day. Just as He took care of the Israelites, He knows what you need and when you need it, and He provides. In a similar way, God knows when your nerves are worn thin or your thoughts become threadbare. He sustains you without any help from you. If you are willing to go where you are called to go and to do what He wants you to do, God will take care of the rest.

Have you felt God calling you to step into new shoes? Have you questioned how you'd find the proper resources if you respond to His call? You can trust God and know for sure that He walks beside you everywhere you go. If you feel God wants you to step into new shoes, trust that He will provide all you need for the next steps in your journey.

Lord, thank You for walking with me and encouraging me to try something new. Help me to listen for Your voice and to be willing to go where You lead. Provide me with guidance and love for each step of the way. I believe in all that You make possible. Amen.

21

What's your Deal Breaker?

If we are thrown into the blazing furnace, the God we serve is able to deliver us from it, and he will deliver us from Your Majesty's hand.

DANIEL 3:17

We set boundaries when we're negotiating a deal. We set the price we're willing to pay for a new car. We set terms for a new job. We impose deal breakers into many decisions because we've established reasonable limits.

The king of Babylon, King Nebuchadnezzar, had ordered that all people in his kingdom must worship a golden idol. The king thought he had a deal breaker when he told Shadrach and his friends—Israelite captives in Babylon—they had to obey the king's orders or he would throw them into a fiery furnace. That would surely make the three Hebrew men agree to anything. What Nebuchadnezzar didn't know was these men trusted that God was at their sides. Some might call this an unreasonable faith—the kind of faith that defies human understanding.

The three men could have compromised their beliefs and worshipped a false god, but this is a deal breaker for God. In the Ten Commandments, God commands that we worship no other gods before Him. The Hebrews knew this, and they refused to worship anyone or anything other than the one true God. They had a deal breaker too.

As you consider the opportunities before you, be sure to set your priorities according to all that God has revealed to you and know your deal breakers. In the same way the men facing the fiery furnace trusted God to save them, you can know God is with you too. All you need is to trust the One who is in control. With His help, you will experience amazing opportunities.

Lord, I know that I usually listen closely in any negotiation. I like to be sure others don't overstep my boundaries. I praise You for helping me set limits and priorities. Thank You for being my one true God and for being by my side every step of the way. Amen.

22

Wisdom and Education

The leaders saw that Peter and John were not afraid to
speak, and they understood that these men had no special
training or education. So they were amazed. Then they
realized that Peter and John had been with Jesus.

ACTS 4:13 NCV

Sometimes we don't achieve our goals. We set them up, but life happens and we let them go, assuming they are gone for good. We assign them a "regrets" status and move on.

Obtaining a formal education is a goal for some people. It certainly was for Nola Ochs, who got her bachelor's degree at the age of ninety-five, graduating from college with her granddaughter. Of course, that wasn't enough for Nola, who went on and got a master's degree as well, graduating when she was ninety-eight. With a perspective few others in her class had, she obtained a degree in history—of which she had lived a good span.

Wally Taibleson, who received his first college degree at the age of seventy, went on to earn three additional bachelor's degrees and graduated from California State University when he was ninety. He said he believed that as long as you were learning, you weren't old.

Perhaps what we should take away from these two golden achievers is that perseverance, initiative, drive, and goals are not strictly for the young. Education may bring you to a certain point, but wisdom carries you beyond your goals; many times they walk hand in hand, one helping the other to become more transparent.

When you're in learning mode, you grow wiser. Peter and John were not well-educated men, but they grew wise through their relationship with Jesus. They learned from a master teacher. The question then is, are you willing to keep growing in wisdom and understanding of all God still has for you? Your willingness to learn motivates your heart and mind and renews your energy and strength.

If you want to grow in any field, there's nothing stopping you. If you want more wisdom, seek God's voice. He never wants you to stop learning. Who knows, there might still be an advanced degree in your future.

Lord, thank You for giving me endless possibility, even when it comes to things I've imagined were beyond my reach. I ask You to educate me in the ways You want me to go. Help me to take steps to accomplish goals that are still mine to fulfill. Amen.

23

Five Years from Now

"For I know the thoughts that I think toward you, says the LORD, thoughts of peace and not of evil, to give you a future and a hope."
JEREMIAH 29:11 NKJV

One common business strategy is to create a five-year plan. The plan allows you to set milestones and assess how you're doing. With each passing year, greater goals will be accomplished. If all goes well, after five years, you will celebrate well-planned growth initiatives.

Sometimes it's tempting to think that achieving success in all of life, not just in business, can happen by considering new options and putting them into a time frame such as a five-year goal-setting plan. However, such planning can often leave out the greatest source of meaning and purpose there is. As a believer, you have the mind of God at your disposal. That means you can start at the top and go to the Creator of the universe to find out what He thinks about you and what you need to succeed. It's not likely He will suggest a five-year plan. It's more likely He will call you to Himself—to an intimate trust relationship with Him that will enable you to take His ordained steps toward achieving your destiny.

When you're twenty-five, imagining a five-year plan is easy. When you're sixty-five, it feels more difficult. Why? Our rational minds believe the person of twenty-five years has a lot more time to achieve her goals. Of course, we don't know the number of our days, and the twenty-five-year-old and the sixty-five-year-old may have the same length of time remaining in their lives. Nevertheless, the hopes and dreams of each are equal in the sight of God.

Imagine that God has greater thoughts, bigger dreams, more hope for your future. Then go and spend time with Him, seek His voice, and know His heart for your work and your life. He promises to give you a future that is rich in hope. His plans are without limit and are not defined by time. He knows that, when you walk with Him, He can work all your life events together for your good and create new possibilities for your future. Are you ready to get going? It's your day to achieve something new!

Lord, I'm timid about stepping out in faith to try something I wanted to do when I was younger. Help me trust that You see me right where I am today and that You know all I can accomplish. I put all my plans and hopes into Your capable hands. Amen.

24

Turning Up the Light

"No one, when he has lit a lamp, puts it in a secret place or under a basket, but on a lampstand, that those who come in may see the light."

LUKE 11:33 NKJV

When journalist Malcolm Muggeridge was asked what he wanted to do with the rest of his life, he answered by saying, "I should like my light to shine, even if only very fitfully, like a match struck in a dark, cavernous night and then flickering out."

One of life's great joys is to be able to offer something meaningful to the world. We want to bring some light into the darkness and make a difference in the lives of others. Muggeridge became a Christian later in life and was an advocate for Mother Teresa. He was amazed by her efforts and the ways that she helped others to shine all around her.

God uses His children as beacons in the world. He turns His face toward us and lets His light shine through us. He knows that by His Spirit we can do amazing things. How we present that light is up to us. We may think our light is too dim to matter or there is nothing we can do to make a difference. We choose to see ourselves as a flickering candle or as a moonbeam. Either way, with God's help, we can turn up the light anytime.

Consider the ways you can brighten someone else's path today. If your faith is alive and well, your light shines in the darkness, and others are drawn to it. Whether you're a beacon on a hill, a bedside table lamp, or even a tiny booklight, your light matters.

Your little light makes it possible for others to discover their own gifts and find their way into God's care and keeping. Never doubt that you were designed to shine. Go, and light up the world with possibility!

Lord of lords, make me willing to set my light on a lampstand, allowing it to light the way for those around me. Help me to stay close to You, learning from You as the Source of all that I can be so that I can shine Your light before others. Amen.

25

The Adventure Continues

*That's right—if you make Insight your priority, and won't take no for
an answer, searching for it like a prospector panning for gold, like an
adventurer on a treasure hunt, believe me, before you know it Fear-
of-God will be yours; you'll have come upon the Knowledge of God.*

PROVERBS 2:3–5 MSG

Perhaps you don't like the idea of living your life as an adventure, as a tale to be told. An adventurous life may take you outside of your comfort zone or cause you to explore risky places. But as a Christian, a life filled with the Spirit of the Creator is an adventure! After all, you're a witness to all that God can do and a reflection of His Light to the world.

You recognize the adventure more fully when you understand what it means to be a child of God. Scripture suggests you're on a road to discovery. You're seeking wisdom and insight, panning for the golden nuggets of God's truth, and hoping to know Him in diverse ways. You're on a lifelong treasure hunt.

No matter your age or where you are professionally or economically, you always have an adventure before you. You are forever invited to turn over new earth, find hidden understanding, and shine a light on new prospects in your thinking. The more you dig up as you study God's Word or understand His presence in your life, the more you'll win the prize: the chance to really know your Lord and Savior.

Some are content to hold the nuggets of truth they received at the beginning of their journey with God, but others suspect there is more to know and more to be revealed in the days ahead. Knowing that God is bigger than your current insights is why you believe your hopes and dreams are still possible!

If you've forgotten where you are on the path, take a new step, and there will be signs ahead that direct you forward. The adventure will continue, and God will walk with you everywhere you go.

Lord, motivate my heart and mind to desire more of You. Help me to seek You like a prospector, patiently looking for nuggets of wisdom, knowing that Your Spirit is the gold just waiting to be discovered. Amen.

26

The Thieves of Possibility

"But know this, that if the master of the house had known
what hour the thief would come, he would have watched
and not allowed his house to be broken into."

LUKE 12:39 NKJV

If you're a list maker, you set priorities, delegate what you can, and do your best to get things done. Urgent needs yell louder for attention, so some items fall through the cracks. You can't do everything! But you need to be sure the really important items don't fall through, because the thieves of possibility are everywhere, ready to distract you.

Create a possibility list, a sacred contract of those things you believe God wants you to accomplish. This is your list of infinite possibility, and God knows that with His help you will do more than you can even imagine. However, like your list of daily chores, you may discover the thieves of possibility throw obstacles in your path, confuse your agenda, or simply make you feel unworthy to accomplish your goals.

Jesus warned us to keep looking up so we can discern those who might get in the way of the work we are meant to do. We don't want thieves to break into our houses and take away our dreams and goals.

One way to bar the door is to pray about your sacred list as often as possible. Pray for guidance and for an understanding of the deliverables. Pray for protection against negative self-talk so worldly opinions don't overshadow you. Pray for diligence to do a little bit each day to move forward with the gifts you've been given.

It's still possible for you to complete those things you and God agreed to do together. It's possible because you are still the apple of His eye and He trusts you to get His work done. Remember, all things are possible with God. May God bless you and keep you in His strength so that you can accomplish remarkable things.

Father God, I am a planner. I make lists of things I need to get done, and sometimes those lists get in the way of the real things I need to do for You. My list of daily chores can be a thief to all I want to do for You. Help me to set You as my first priority. Amen.

27

What a Mess!

Enthusiasm without knowledge is not good. If you
act too quickly, you might make a mistake.

PROVERBS 19:2 NCV

Perhaps you think the desires of your heart are no longer possible because you've made too many mistakes in your life. You feel like you're stuck and nothing can change. Victor Hugo said, "Great blunders are often made, like large ropes, of a multitude of fibers." If you've been gathering the mistakes you've made in life one fiber at a time, you may indeed have created a mess, a chord that seems unbreakable. You may wonder if it's still possible to untangle your past and start again.

The answer lies not so much in the measure of your mistakes but in the condition of your heart. There's nothing God likes better than a contrite heart. After all, when you're sorry for the mistakes you've made, you're ready to be remolded and shaped into something that better resembles who God has created you to be. You want to change, and you know you need God's help to do so. We read in 1 John 1:9 that if we confess our sins, God is faithful and just and will forgive us our sins and purify us from all unrighteousness. Wow! That's quite a promise!

If you've confessed your messy life to God, He can do something miraculous with it. He can purify you. He can give you a clean slate. He can make your plans and dreams possible again. Not only *can* He do that, but He *will* do that. He promises to purify you and let you try again.

Chances are you didn't get past your toddler years without making a few mistakes. As you got older those mistakes were compounded by poor choices and misunderstandings. God gives you the chance to open your heart and share your brokenness so you can grow into the person you were always meant to be. Praise God for giving you divine possibility to accomplish great things. Turn those old ropes into bridges, and move on into the blessings God has just for you.

Lord, You amaze me. I can hardly take in the gift of Your forgiveness. I know I don't deserve it. I am grateful to You for cleansing my heart and offering me a fresh start. You make me feel like anything is possible as long as I stick close to You! Amen.

28

Sticky Self-Talk

Above all else, guard your heart, for everything you
do flows from it. Keep your mouth free of perversity;
keep corrupt talk far from your lips.

PROVERBS 4:23–24

There may be nothing more poisonous than the negative stories we carry in our heads. We recall unkind remarks from childhood, when we were too young to defend our psyches from the experience, and the words continue to wound us. Words are powerful things.

One writer said we have to be careful about our thoughts because those thoughts eventually seek a voice. Once words are spoken, they become actions, and if those actions are repeated too often, they become habits. Before we know it, those habits have set up house within our hearts and minds, becoming patterns of behavior that establish our character. Avoid becoming a person driven by bad habits and unkind words, driven by thoughts you can no longer erase from your mind.

Proverbs warns us to be protective of our hearts because it is from the heart that everything else flows. When we look to

God to guard our hearts, we know He offers swift protection. He sustains our souls, remolds our character, and renews our possibilities for future good.

The best way for life to overflow with possibility is to turn your thoughts toward thanking and praising God. The more you spend time with God, the more it becomes a regular habit. He alone can shape your character and help you become all you hope to be. He offers you infinite possibility, and nothing will get in the way of the things He wants to accomplish through you.

If you've allowed negative talk from your childhood to stick to your heart and mind, turn it over to God. Let Him wipe those thoughts out of your mind, replacing unkind words with love and peace. When you do, you'll discover all that is still possible for you through your heavenly Creator!

Lord, thank You for sticking by me. I've carried a lot of baggage around through the years. I've suffered because of ugly words, and I ask You to wipe them away. Guard my heart and mind in Christ Jesus. Amen.

29

Understanding God's Yes

*"All you need to say is simply 'Yes' or 'No'; anything
beyond this comes from the evil one."*

MATTHEW 5:37

ou've probably heard it said in regard to prayer that God's answers are either yes, no, or maybe, but when you're trying to connect with God about the things that are still possible in your life, you want a clear yes or no answer.

Matthew concludes that those who offer more than yes or no may well slip into ulterior motives or some kind of negative spin. Clearly there is something significant about being confident and straightforward. If you're a parent, you probably learned early on that it was important for your *yes* to mean yes and your *no* to mean no. Otherwise, house rules were always open to further discussion. *Yes* and *no,* then, are big words indeed!

Consider the times God has said yes that have made a tremendous difference in your life. He said, "Yes, I accept you and love you and forgive you when you trust Me and believe in My Son, Jesus." His yes is unconditional. His yes is for eternity, and nothing will change His mind about His response to you. God's promises to you are all yes statements.

We might say, "It's impossible!" God says, "All things are possible with Me." We might say, "Nobody loves me." God says, "I love you, and just to prove it I offer you redemption and forgiveness." We might say, "I'm so afraid." God says, "I have not given you a spirit of confusion or fear. I am with you always" (2 Timothy 1:7; Matthew 28:20).

God's yes means only one thing. He is there. He is the author of all that is still possible in your life. Just let Him know that you trust Him to be there for you and that you believe He makes all things possible.

Lord, I sometimes say yes when I'm not sure I should. Help me to be more confident and honest when I offer a promise to someone else. Help me to be bold any time I say yes to You. Amen.

30

Imagine That!

With God's power working in us, God can do much,
much more than anything we can ask or imagine.

EPHESIANS 3:20 NCV

One of the slogans of a large regional bank near my home asks, "What would you like the power to do?" It's an interesting question, and perhaps our first thought would be something like, "I'd like the power to make money appear in my bank account."

Now consider that question with a spiritual bias. What would you like the power of God to do for you? Maybe we'd say something like, "I'd like God to make it possible for me to . . ." You fill in the blank.

The difference is that the bank can ask that question and the answer totally depends on your power. You are the catalyst that must get things done and make things change for the better. You can spend less and save more, and your bank account will indeed grow.

On the other hand, as a spiritual question, the only one who can truly affect the outcome is God. He is the only one with the power to protect your hopes and dreams and give you opportunities that take you past anything you can ask or imagine.

What prevents you from dreaming of doing things that are literally impossible? If we accept the verse from Ephesians, we see that God's power isn't a force beyond us that we can't reach. It's a force that works within us, and the more we open up to it, the more possibility it brings to our lives.

God can out-imagine you any day of the week. He can orchestrate changes and opportunities in your life that your mind would never conceive, much less believe to be possible.

Talk to God about shaping your imagination. When you do, God will give you powerful opportunities from His abundant treasures.

Creator God, You used Your imagination to create the whole world. No human being could ever have imagined a platypus or a weeping willow. We need Your power working within us to do ordinary things and extraordinary things and Your imagination to understand all that is still possible. Amen.

31

You're a Star!

He counts the stars and names each one.

PSALM 147:4 NCV

ou probably don't think of yourself as a star. Twinkling stars show up in the darkness. They remind people that God is in the heavens watching over them. Stars bring joy to everything around them. But you are a star because you shine your light on the world as well.

Remembering that you're a star reminds you of your purpose. You know you have a job to do, and nothing can keep you from accomplishing it. You shine with possibility and you never doubt your calling. With God's help, you shine with infinite possibility and are called to a glorious purpose. Look up to the heavens and remind yourself: you are God's handiwork just like the constellations above.

All of creation signals God's desire to fill our lives with promise and hope. It is a living example of what God did and continues to do to sustain life and make new things possible. Psalm 139 reminds you that God knit you in your mother's womb. He knew you before you were born. He knew what He intended for your life and He never makes mistakes.

Take another look at those goals, dreams, and hopes you left behind and see if they still have luster. They may seem dimmer than when they first appeared, but that doesn't mean they were never meant to be. It doesn't mean God never intended for you to polish them up and make them shine.

Ask God what you might do with your earlier bits of stardust. After all, the One who counts the stars and calls them by name knows exactly what you need to help you shine.

You are an amazing reflection of Jesus' light.

Father in heaven, I marvel at stars. I love to see them sparkle in the night sky, giving glory to the darkness. I love the thought that I might shine into some dark corners here on earth. Help me to believe You have many ways to set me aglow once more. Amen.

32

Exercise Your Spirit

*Training your body helps you in some ways, but
serving God helps you in every way by bringing you
blessings in this life and in the future life, too.*

1 TIMOTHY 4:8 NCV

ost of us are pretty health conscious. We try to eat well
and get some exercise and a reasonable amount of sleep.
We know it's the best way to keep our earthly vessels from wearing out too quickly. If we do it enough, we form a habit that becomes part of our lifestyle, something we rarely have to think about.

Imagine what would happen if you applied those same strategies to your spiritual life. What if you decided to be soul conscious? If you were, you would look for ways to feed your soul, put what you've learned into action, exercise the joy of the Lord, and rest in God's presence. Before long, they would become spiritual habits that make a difference in your life, restoring your earthly vessel—heart and mind and soul.

You can exercise your faith. Ask God for things you believe are impossible. Feed your dreams. Bring them back to the light of day, reinventing them or spinning them in a way you never imagined before. Shape them and buff them up so they are fit to go out into the world. These are the things you can still do.

Then let them rest. Surrender them to God's creative, powerful, and mighty hands. God knows what's important to you. Desires of your heart are not fleeting fantasies; they are key to your existence. They nourish your spirit and bring joy to your soul.

It's a great day to exercise. Push forward with God's help and lift up your hands to Him in praise. He will reveal the paths that lead to new possibilities. You can count on it!

Lord, I am truly awed by the things You do. Though I believed that some of my hopes and dreams were long gone, You reminded me of their possibility. Thank You for nourishing me with Your Spirit. Amen.

33

Been There! Done That!

Being strengthened with all power according to his glorious
might so that you may have great endurance and patience.
COLOSSIANS 1:11

It is easy to sabotage your own possibilities. As you pursue your goals, someone may offer helpful advice you've heard before. If you've already tried some version of their suggestion, you dismiss it, saying, "Been there, done that!" But is there a chance that something that didn't work before could work now and is worth considering again? Could it be possible that with just a little more initial perseverance the advice might have even worked the first time?

Experience is a helpful teacher, but you are putting obstacles in your own path when you dismiss any tactic that didn't work for you in the past. Things could turn out very differently this time.

Jesus shared the story of a great man who prepared a dinner and sent invitations through his servants for people to come to his table, and he discovered that many of them made excuses not to come. The banquet was ready, the invitations were sent, but the people refused to come. Of course, Jesus wanted His hearers to understand that this is precisely what God does. He invites us to come to His table, to be nourished and fed by His Spirit, and yet we make excuses not to come. We don't recognize that God is continually giving us opportunities to join Him and share in His bounty.

Do you dismiss opportunities that feel familiar, thinking you tried them before? If you do, go back to the Lord's table and seek His presence and advice. Ask if He is opening a door that was once closed because the timing is better now. You have changed too, and that alone could make all the difference.

If you resist moving forward because you think you've been there before, don't make the excuse of "been there, done that." Instead, ask for God's endurance and patience to wait for His new way to be revealed where none existed before.

Lord, thank You for giving me another chance to move forward and to succeed at something I have long held dear. Help me listen for Your voice and move in the direction You would have me go, even if I think I've tried it before. In Jesus' name, I pray. Amen.

34

Getting Off the Fence

"Why can't you decide for yourselves what is right?"

LUKE 12:57 NCV

*H*ave you ever sat on the proverbial fence, unable to decide which way you should go? Maybe like Tevye in the story of the *Fiddler on the Roof,* you are almost ready to choose from one hand when you realize that "on the other hand," another choice could make more sense. You simply can't decide what to do.

Sometimes God is ready to move forward and give you a life full of all the possibility you've imagined. He's just waiting for you to get off the fence and actually choose to embrace it. He's patiently waiting for you to catch up and be ready once He says it's time to act.

The fence is not particularly comfortable. What's worse is that, while you're on the fence, you're assured to go nowhere. The fence offers momentary safety but no safety net, so it can't really protect you. At some point, you'll fall off. Whichever way you tumble, the decision will be made.

There is a better way. You could take your tough decisions to God and share with Him why it is so hard to make a good choice.

As you lay the options out before Him, He may make it clear what to do. Just talking to Him may chase the fog of indecision away.

Choose one option and stick with it. Once you do, it could be surprising how quickly your possibilities loom before you. You may be able to get off the fence once and for all.

When it comes to decision-making, Theodore Roosevelt said, "In any moment of decision the best thing you can do is the right thing, the next best thing is the wrong thing, and the worst thing is to do nothing."

Sitting on the fence will never be the right decision. To know what is still possible may require you to make new choices. Sit down with God and He will hear your concerns and bless you with a sense of direction.

Lord, I know that I procrastinate. I wait for the right time or the right set of circumstances to guide me into a new direction. I pray You will be my guide and help me to get off the fence so I can move into new possibility. Amen.

35

Going Back to Square One

So let us go on to grown-up teaching. Let us not go back
over the beginning lessons we learned about Christ.

HEBREWS 6:1 NCV

Sometimes you work really hard, gain momentum, and feel like you're on the right track. Everything is going along great, and then it screeches to a halt. Your boss says to switch gears because something more important has come up, so yesterday's urgent project is put on a back burner. Your doctor says you need to rest because you've been working too hard and it's time to take a break, but resting is the last thing you want to do. The money you planned to use for a vacation is now needed to cover an unexpected bill. You're back to square one!

But life isn't a linear map. Even though you're feeling like you have to start over, your dreams may not be in plain sight, but they could be closer than you think. A small amount of effort connected to God's powerlines can catapult you forward.

When you first started learning about God, it was okay to be on square one. You needed basic teaching and understanding. You needed to learn who He is before you could have a sense of where He wants you to go. But eventually, both you and God became invested in moving you forward. And now, when you have setbacks, you don't have to go all the way back to the beginning.

As it turns out, that dynamic has never changed. You are still learning about God and getting to know more clearly what He wants from you. You are a grown-up child of His now, and He trusts you to be equipped and ready to do His work even after you take a few steps back in your progress.

Look at the dreams you've achieved in your life and see if God has more possibilities looming in them. Maybe you will discover something new, a gem of what is still possible.

Since we never bother to number the squares after square one, you can just decide what square you think you're on and then take two steps forward. You're on to infinite possibilities.

Lord, I pray that I won't spend so much time looking back at the things I hoped would happen in the past that I miss the opportunities You have in front of me now. Shine a light on those things I need to grasp so I can keep making progress. Thank You for continuing to help me grow and move on. Amen.

36

Seeking with Earnestness, Diligence, and Perseverance

"Ask, and God will give to you. Search, and you will find.
Knock, and the door will open for you. Yes, everyone who
asks will receive. Everyone who searches will find. And
everyone who knocks will have the door opened."

MATTHEW 7:7–8 NCV

I f you ever worry about the future, how you will make ends meet or find the meaning and purpose you desire, these two verses are the ones to hold on to. They speak about seeking God's provision for your every need. The use of the three words "ask," "search," and "knock" underscore that our seeking is to be done with earnestness, diligence, and perseverance—with a "never give up" and "keep on keeping on" attitude.

Our first step is just to ask. The verses say if you ask, God will give. That means God will react. He'll do something. He'll be there. It may not always be exactly what you expect or what you think you want, but it will always be what God knows is best for you. It will be consistent with His will and what He Himself has promised to give.

Also, if you search, then you will find. What will you find? You'll find answers or direction or those things that God wants you to know and do.

Finally, the passage says that if you knock, the door will open for you. It doesn't say that you'll knock and nobody will be home or that you'll knock and the door will be locked. It says that all you have to do is knock and the door will open. When the door opens, you are going to be standing in the presence of the only one who can actually answer your questions or do something about your dilemma. You'll be face-to-face with God, the One you asked for help.

In two short verses, God promises that He will provide for all your needs—that He knows how to give good gifts to His children (Matthew 7:11). So what will you do with that guarantee? First, trust that when you persevere and expect God's guidance in your "asking, searching, and knocking," you will "receive, find, or have a door open." Once God opens the door, you discover the One who knows what you need and invites you in to experience His grace and receive His guidance.

Lord, I am standing at Your door, humbly prepared to ask for Your help. I pray I will listen to You and allow You to open new doors to what is yet to be. Amen.

37

What Should You Do Now?

But when you ask, you must believe and not doubt, because the one
who doubts is like a wave of the sea, blown and tossed by the wind.

JAMES 1:6

Life is full of turning points. Once you graduate from high school, you find yourself immersed in the question: *What should I do with my life?* You may go to college, get a job, or perhaps join the military.

However, some of the turning points in your life won't be ones you planned. They will shake your world up and remind you that you're not in control.

When you receive a difficult medical diagnosis, find yourself in divorce court, or come to the realization that your career path is not working well for you, you have to seek new possibilities. You have to turn to the One who knows your future and trust Him.

This letter from James reminds you that when you go to God to figure out what you should do next, you have to believe He has the answer and that He is willing to share that answer with you.

You have to believe without any doubt that God knows the way you should go.

Scripture says that if you have doubt instead of faith, you'll be like a wave that is blown about and tossed by the wind. You'll be rising and falling, flooded with worries and swept away with your concerns. You'll need a life preserver.

But when you put all things in God's hand, He calms the waves of uncertainty and brings peace to your heart. He helps you stay afloat and assures your survival.

God wants you to realize that with Him, peace is still possible. With Him, opportunities abound. He has set you on a firm foundation of faith so that He can help you when everything around you is scary. Let your soul be at peace in His powerful hands today.

Lord, thank You for steadying me through the waves of doubt. Help me to stay strong, and fill me with belief in all that You have for me. Grant me peace today, Lord, so that I stand on the solid rock of faith as we determine the best direction for me to go. Amen.

38

Attempt the Impossible

And without faith it is impossible to please God, because
anyone who comes to him must believe that he exists
and that he rewards those who earnestly seek him.

HEBREWS 11:6

ritish theologian and Baptist preacher F. B. Meyer wrote, "We never test the resources of God until we attempt the impossible."

If you do a quick survey of your life, how many times would you be able to note that you "attempted the impossible"? Perhaps you took a few chances or did some things that were a bit risky, but how often did you rely solely on God to move forward?

Most of us have been trained from an early age to be self-reliant. We're nurtured to be independent and expected to take care of ourselves. Chances are, you've been pretty good at finding ways to provide for your well-being and that of the people around you. Your work is pleasing to God and your faith has grown in the process.

To determine what is still possible for you, start by looking at what is impossible for you. What would it take, even now, for you to attempt the impossible? What kind of faith would you need to believe so much in God's existence and power that nothing could hold you back?

We must challenge ourselves to seek things we know we cannot do on our own. If we attempt those new things in our humanness, we will fail miserably. The only hope we have, then, is for God to intervene, step up to the plate, and help us develop our swing. Only then will we see the ball, the object of our hopes and dreams, go sailing high in the sky over the outfield and on to victory.

The challenge is not simply to wonder what is still possible, but to actively seek God's help to do those things that have been unavailable in the past. Have faith in all that He can do. Impossible things will happen.

Lord of the Possible, help me to be truly unsatisfied with the commonplace and the ordinary, those things that I can do with my eyes closed and without thinking twice. Help me step up and step out in faith in bigger ways, totally trusting You for the outcome. Amen.

39

Invisible Support

Now to the King eternal, immortal, invisible, the only
God, be honor and glory for ever and ever. Amen.
1 TIMOTHY 1:17

God is your invisible means of support. You may have people in your life who offer moral support, emotional support, and maybe even financial support, but not one of those people can support you quite the way God can. You hear His voice in your heart and soul, and you trust that He walks with you each day.

When faith convicts you of God's presence, it raises the bar of your belief system. It taps into those things that seem impossible for others and reminds you that nothing in this world is God's equal. You believe the unbelievable because you've witnessed it with your own eyes. You've seen people healed of diseases, witnessed someone's triumph over drug abuse, and noticed God's hand at work in ways that no human being could accomplish alone.

As a faithful witness to the invisible God and as a believer in the unbelievable, you are a prime candidate to receive the impossible. You make room for God in places where others have already shut the door. You know His name, and He knows yours. It's a mutual friendship and a relationship you both count on.

When you doubt that good things are still possible for you, call on the God of your heart—the Invisible, the Invincible, and the Everlasting. He supplies all your needs. It's an amazing dynamic that only those with eyes to see and ears to hear can understand. Some rely on virtual reality or stories they see on reality TV, but you know there is only one reality: the reality of Jesus, the Son of God, holding the door open for you. You have an incredible means of support. To God be the glory!

Lord God, I know You are supernatural, invisible, and unable to be seen face-to-face, and I trust You. You have spoken to my heart, helped me to recognize Your hand at work in my life, and healed me of my brokenness. Help me move forward into all that is still possible. Amen.

40

Obstacle Courses

We know that in everything God works for the good of those who love him. They are the people he called, because that was his plan.
ROMANS 8:28 NCV

We might imagine that we'd enjoy life more if there were fewer obstacles for us to maneuver and more straight paths. After all, we just want to get where we're going.

However, the problem is that we get bored easily and tend to stray from easy paths that don't challenge our minds. Human beings are natural problem solvers. We enjoy the idea that life experience and rational thought will provide the answers to whatever problems we're facing.

If that's true, we have no reason to feel frustrated when our plans don't come together or our paths are suddenly bombarded with obstacles blocking us from our goals. The twists and turns on the road ahead should make it more interesting.

But when you're close to the goal, the last thing you want is one more hurdle to overcome. You just want to get to the finish line. Now the game is no longer fun, and that obstacle feels like the end of your possibilities.

God's road is littered with twists and turns, and they are intentional. On one hand, they help you remember you can't travel far without checking in with Him. They also remind you that you are not in control. Since God is working everything out for your good, He likes you to stay close to Him. If you stray, you're apt to bump into one unknown difficulty after another because you took your eyes off the Guide.

Your dreams are still possible, but you have to focus on the direction God gives you. To get to your personal goal in the most direct way, you must keep your eyes on Jesus so He can shine a light on all possibilities.

It's time to walk forward boldly with your head held high.

Lord, I am so grateful that You planned my path for me. Give me wisdom to follow You and not get sidetracked by things that might lead me in the wrong direction. Help me to stay on the course You designed for me. Amen.

41

Adjusting Your Sails

But He said to them, "Why are you fearful, O you of
little faith?" Then He arose and rebuked the winds
and the sea, and there was a great calm.

MATTHEW 8:26 NKJV

Some days, it feels like you wake up sailing into a storm. Everything was peaceful when you went to sleep, but out of nowhere, a storm arose and everything in your world starts rocking. As you become more conscious of your situation, your fears mount. You get wet feet as you try to figure out what to do next, and you consider bailing.

It's tempting on days like that to simply go back to sleep and hope things look better when you wake up again. It's tempting but not helpful. After all, you don't want to drown in the downpour of the mess around you, so you get to work.

It's important to know when and how to adjust your sails to get the maximum benefit of the prevailing winds. One of the quickest adjustments is making that mental shift from staring at the problems to reaching out to the Divine Captain of your ship. John Calvin wrote, "Seeing that a Pilot steers the ship in which we sail, who will never allow us to perish even in the midst of shipwrecks, there is no reason why our minds should be overwhelmed with fear and overcome with weariness."

In other words, we have to reach up to the One who can rebuke the winds of calamity and seek His direction. When you do, the winds will become less threatening, and the gray skies will begin to clear.

Oh, it's not magic. It doesn't happen because you wish it would. It happens because you adjusted your sails and gave God the opportunity to help steer you to the clearing.

It's not especially fashionable to try calling out to the Lord, but it's always the place to start. After you've done that, look up resources and ideas on the Internet, post an urgent request on your Facebook page, or meet with your close advisors. Those are resources God gives us to find answers to our problems, but they are secondary to Him. Don't look at the darkening clouds of despair; just get knee-deep in prayer. The God of your heart knows where the winds blow best to get you where you need to go.

Lord, when I feel threatened, my first inclination is to find the answers myself, to fix the problems as best as I can. Help me to adjust the sails of my thinking and turn everything over to you. Only You know all that is possible in the situations I face. Amen.

42

A Legacy of Possibilities

And whatever you do, do it heartily, as to the Lord and not
to men, knowing that from the Lord you will receive the
reward of the inheritance; for you serve the Lord Christ.
COLOSSIANS 3:23–24 NKJV

Each of us is a builder. We may not put in a foundation that will create a skyscraper, but the impact of our work may be just as strong. It may last for generations, creating our legacy to the planet. The thing about a beautiful hotel or incredible symphony hall is that they were each built the same way. There was an architect with a vision for the work. There were blueprints and scaffolds, engineers and carpenters, all with an eye for what needed to be done. What was impossible for any one of them alone was brought to life by all of them together.

You are the architect of your life experiences. You had the vision, conceived the possibility, and found the right people to create the work. At times you were part of the crew, making someone else's vision possible. You've contributed to the well-being of friends and family and encouraged those who could no longer see what was possible. You've been creating a legacy of possibilities your entire life.

God has been nudging your steps, directing your path, and helping you move forward. He has worked with you to create a lasting legacy by the things you do and the people you move closer to the light of His love.

Samuel Johnson wrote about the building of a palace. He said, "Great works are performed, not by strength, but by perseverance; yonder palace was raised by single stones, yet you see its height and spaciousness." In other words, great things are accomplished one step at a time, and our only job as builders of possibility is to stick with it.

May God bless the work of your hands and heart as you keep building His legacy one loving step at a time.

Lord, I never thought of myself as a builder in this way, but I love the idea that I can do small things, one at a time, to help further the work of Your kingdom. Thank You for equipping me to do those things that may bless the lives of others with new possibility. Amen.

43

Write Your Own Story

Beautiful words fill my mind. I am speaking of royal
things. My tongue is like the pen of a skilled writer.

PSALM 45:1 NCV

Every day you're adding another chapter to your story. You're filling the pages of your life with memories and experiences. Some of your ideas and the stories you've told along the way have impacted others and forged new possibilities.

Words and ideas can be beautiful, as they were to King David in the psalm above. Other times, they can disparage, belittle, and prove difficult, sending negativity into someone's story that lasts for years. Words are powerful and create harmony or discord.

As you write your own story, how will you imagine your possibilities? If you're thinking opportunities have passed you by and there's nothing you can do to bring them back, you may echo the words of John Greenleaf Whittier when he wrote, "Of all sad words of tongue or pen, the saddest are these, 'It might have been.'"

But the Bible tells us God makes us new every morning. That means each day brings its own chance for amazing things to happen. Each day you choose to reflect the optimism of King David or the sadness of Whittier. Your story is unfolding, and it can be everything you want it to be as long as you dedicate it to the author of your life and seek His face to endorse your efforts.

Your story is important. It's an adventure with dynamic characters and villains, inevitable drama, and surprising happiness. It has victories and defeat. Everything about it prepares you for all that God intends. He equips you through the ups and downs, showing you the way to make better choices. He knows that with every breath you take, opportunity and possibility are built in.

Perhaps the best words for today are the words of praise you lift up to God for all He is still doing to bless you and keep you and help you be strong. God is always near, ready to help you create a beautiful life story.

Lord, help me to listen for what You would have me know, pondering the words You've given me in the Bible to strengthen and renew me in body, mind, and spirit. Thank You, Lord, for setting me on this incredible journey. Amen.

44

Because God Loves You

*And hope does not put us to shame, because God's
love has been poured out into our hearts through
the Holy Spirit, who has been given to us.*

ROMANS 5:5

How big does your heart have to be for you to receive the love God is willing to pour into it? Would a cup fill you up? Would a bucket cause your spirit to overflow with joy? What about a fire hose, drawing from the ocean? If you had that much of God's love pouring into your heart, would that help you see Him more clearly and desire to please Him in every way?

Well, get ready then! Your heart is not big enough to take in the amount of love God has already poured into you through the Holy Spirit. You are still unable or unwilling to let it flow in because it seems too hard for you to understand. After all, you're a sinner! How could God love you that much?

Remember the verse in Matthew 19:26 that says, "With God all things are possible" (NIV)? Have you stopped to consider what that really means? It would be difficult to create an exhaustive list of its implications, but here are a few of them.

Despite your failings, your stubbornness, and your unwillingness to surrender your total heart and mind to Him, God doesn't give up. He won't leave you in a stew of misery. It means that when God looks at you, He doesn't see the tumult and chaos you have created, but instead, He sees the opportunity to draw you closer to Him. He sees that with the love of His Son, who paid for all your errors in judgment and your rebelliousness, there still exists a chance for the two of you to build an amazing relationship. God will take you and love you into a perfect existence, His existence.

If knowing you are loved that much doesn't help you realize possibilities exist all around you, it's hard to say what could do it. You've been redeemed and loved into being a child of God from now through eternity. Grab hold of His possibilities and your heart will grow bigger and bigger. Let your spirit rejoice in Him today.

Lord, You give me love that is unconditional and undeserved. You let me know You are near me. Help me receive You in my heart and in my spirit in ways that I've never been able to before. Help me to love You right back! Amen.

45

Going to the Well

Jacob's well was there, and Jesus, tired as he was from the journey,
sat down by the well. It was about noon. When a Samaritan woman
came to draw water, Jesus said to her, "Will you give me a drink?"
JOHN 4:6–7

Have you ever had an unexpected conversation with a stranger that resonated with you for months, causing you to wonder about its meaning? Perhaps you met while you were traveling, talked about the scenery, and then the person left you with a parting comment that intrigued you, perhaps even changed your perspective.

As you think about random conversations, imagine the Samaritan woman's surprise when she went to draw water from Jacob's well. This was her daily routine, and nothing of importance ever happened until the day a strange man asked her for water. As they talked, she realized He knew everything about her even though she had never met Him before. It was baffling.

The Samaritan woman thought her life story had already been written. She knew the poor life choices she had made and that she was an outcast in her own culture. She knew the possibilities for a good future were slim to none.

When she met Jesus, she became dreadfully aware of her poor decisions and of the mess she had made of her life. She was aware that this man knew her story as though He had read every page with interest. It was as if He hoped to meet her so that they could talk. She realized this encounter was more important than any she had ever had. The conversation changed her life, and the next time she went back to the well she was a different person. She was filled with Living Water.

This might be one of the most important "chance" encounters ever recorded. Why? Because the Samaritan woman lived in a world with no possibilities, and Jesus showed her that the impossible was possible after all.

Jesus is still meeting people where they are. Great things are possible when we choose to follow His Light.

Lord, please help me to recognize You anytime we meet. Help me to invite You into my life every day and not just wait for a chance meeting. I ask You to remind me of who I am in You and of all that is still possible in my life. Amen.

46

The Doughnut or the Hole

"This is why I use stories to teach the people: They see, but they don't really see. They hear, but they don't really hear or understand."

MATTHEW 13:13 NCV

The Optimist's Creed is a whimsical saying that was printed in medieval-style art on every box of Mayflower Donuts from the 1930s through the 1970s. This personal motto of founder Adolph Levitt read: "As you ramble on through life, brother, whatever be your goal, keep your eye upon the doughnut, and not upon the hole."

Whether you see the doughnut or the hole, or perhaps a combination of the two, tells a lot about your personality style. An optimist believes that good will prevail and setbacks are temporary. As believers, they are people who look to God for the things they don't understand, trusting He has all the answers to the secrets of life. Generally speaking, they will be the ones who see the doughnut every time, preferably with chocolate sprinkles on top.

Jesus told stories in parables, or word pictures. He used local surroundings and household objects to illustrate His points. He hoped by doing so, listeners would understand the point He was making. He offered them a new perspective. Perhaps if He were with us today, He would use this little poem about the doughnut and the hole to make a point about the way we perceive things. His stories were designed to help people think differently.

Research shows that people with an optimistic lens tend to stay healthier, embrace others with respect and joy, and imagine a brighter future. They believe God is in control. They walk around obstacles and look for opportunities. Winston Churchill said, "A pessimist sees the difficulty in every opportunity; an optimist sees the opportunity in every difficulty."

Optimists have hope. Hope lives on possibilities, trusting that those things that are meant to be will come to be.

You may need a healthy dose of reality to get through life, but your reality can be tempered by your willingness to believe the One who provided the doughnut in the first place, meaning for sweet things to come your way.

Father of Hope, it is not always easy to recognize possibilities still exist as I try to imagine the future. Please open my eyes to see You in new ways and to hear You with new ears. I have unending hope because You reign. Amen.

47

Pie in the Sky

In Him you also trusted, after you heard the word of truth,
the gospel of your salvation; in whom also, having believed,
you were sealed with the Holy Spirit of promise.

EPHESIANS 1:13 NKJV

Remember when you were a kid and you could make a promise with a "pinkie swear"? You just had to lock pinkie fingers, and somehow you believed that sealed the deal. You made a promise that you would keep it. Until you didn't, of course.

Culturally, we love the idea that we can make choices to freely discover the path most suited to our gifts and talents. The only problem is that our paths are strewn with broken promises, empty vessels that were never filled. We lost faith in anything that seemed too ideal, and hope vanished with our youth.

A pinkie promise may well have been a bit "pie in the sky" with nothing to support it, but those promises pale in comparison to the way God makes promises. God makes promises that remain true for eternity. He never changes the terms of what He has agreed to, and that makes Him trustworthy.

How can you take hold of the future and have faith in its

possibilities? Perhaps one answer is to cling to the truth. After all, you were sealed with the Holy Spirit of promise. A seal is the ultimate "pinkie swear." A seal represents an undeniable fact. If you've been sealed by the Holy Spirit, you have full access to all the authority of heaven. You have rights and privileges that last forever because the promise will never be broken.

When promises fall apart, you always have a place to go— to the One who has signed, sealed, and delivered you from sin and who loves you beyond measure. God offers you possibilities and hope beyond the rainbow. You can trust that He has more for you.

Lord, broken promises are everywhere I go. They drain the hope out of my life and make me wonder if anything is yet possible. I pray for Your face to shine upon me and show me what You would have me do. I promise to do my best to honor any agreement we make. I pinkie swear! Amen.

48

In Praise of Little Things

"If you cannot do even the little things, then
why worry about the big things?"
LUKE 12:26 NCV

It's probable that no two people think of little things and big things in the same way. After all, what seems like a small thing to you may be extraordinary to someone else. Review the little things you've created, overcome, or managed in your life that brought you to today. Sometimes little things give you clues as to what else is possible.

For example, if you love to bake a loaf of homemade bread when someone new comes to your church, then baking, creating, or giving may be your sphere of opportunity. It's a source of fulfillment and pride. It's a little thing that, for you, has a big payoff. The idea is to take a look at the things you do that give you a sense of joy and see if there's an opportunity to build a greater possibility.

When Jesus invited the disciples to join Him in His work, they didn't know exactly what to expect. They weren't highly educated, but they exhibited useful skills as fishermen and tax collectors. He took them from where they were and helped them become extraordinary men. He saw something in them that they likely would never have seen in themselves, and He gave them new direction. He invited them to "follow" Him, and in doing so, they discovered new and important truths about themselves.

Possibilities are not always elusive dreams you have hooked to a shining star. Sometimes they are the little things you do every day that can be changed into big acts of faith.

You're invited to "follow" in God's plans for you in a new way. Seek His direction to act with even greater gusto in the years ahead. After all, when God sees what you can do, He opens the doors to new opportunities. It's a good day to think bigger, and maybe even bigger than that.

Lord, help me to see what You would encourage me to do from here. I know that whatever I do to serve You is always a big thing because You make it so. I pray I will not overlook the opportunities I have to develop activities, hobbies, and special talents that could create new possibilities in the future. Amen.

49

Your Possibility Parachute

Trust the LORD with all your heart, and don't depend
on your own understanding. Remember the LORD
in all you do, and he will give you success.

PROVERBS 3:5–6 NCV

Remember the trust game you played at camp where you were supposed to close your eyes and fall backward? You had to trust that the people behind you would actually catch you and not let you fall. It was a simple exercise, but the point was well taken. You've probably looked for the people meant to stand behind you and hold you up ever since.

In your search for new possibilities, perhaps even divine possibilities, you have to trust God has more for you. When someone dons a parachute and jumps out of an airplane, they don't *hope* the parachute will open. They don't *hope* the odds are in their favor that the parachute will open. They *trust* the parachute works and that they will land safely on the ground.

Imagine you are seeking God's possibilities for you. You believe that you trust Him. However, when you pick up the parachute of possibility, you can't quite convince yourself it will open.

You believe the parachute should work, but something holds you back from taking that leap of faith. You have trouble believing God is there when you're out on the skinny branches of your faith.

Proverbs tells you to trust the Lord with all your heart. That means you must let go of negative self-talk. You have to look past where you've been and give yourself a chance to fly free, gently moving in a new direction.

God has blessed you with incredible talents and skills. He has given you a parachute of possibility that will open every time if you trust Him with all your heart. He is always there to catch you if you fall.

You may never jump from an airplane, but when you look up and seek new fulfilling possibilities, trust that God is with you. All you need to do is take a leap of faith.

Lord, I believe all things are possible through and with You. However, I have to admit when You ask me to trust that You are my parachute, I hesitate a little more than I should. Help me to trust You and not hold anything back. I know when I do that wonderful things are still possible! Amen.

50

Simply Magical Thinking

Using their tricks, the magicians tried to do the same thing,
but they could not make the dust change into gnats.

EXODUS 8:18 NCV

Perhaps when you were a child, you remember reading the book *The Wonderful Wizard of Oz* by L. Frank Baum. It is full of imaginative and sometimes scary scenes. Kids moved on to *The Chronicles of Narnia* by C. S. Lewis and J. R. R. Tolkien's great wizard Gandalf in *The Lord of the Rings*. Today kids are entranced with J. K. Rowling's fantasy world of the wizards of Hogwarts in the Harry Potter series.

Every time and culture has its own version of the witches and warlocks who cause us to shiver even when we try not to buy into their stories. Even the Old Testament has stories of magicians who try to outdo God's power. These characters eventually recognize their limitations. They live on magical thinking that has no foundation at all.

So what about you? As you ponder future possibilities, what's your approach? Do you hope like Dorothy that you'll find a wizard who can solve your problems so you can go home again? Do you imagine a Harry Potter-like hero who will emerge victorious with a magic spell? Or do you stand with Moses, knowing there is no power that compares with God's power?

Your future depends on what you accept as truth. Your possibilities are endless when you stand before God and trust Him to give you the right perspective.

Magical thinking is important as a child, and in some measure it's still important to the childlike faith you have now. The difference is there's only one God who has all the power—only one truth. "With God all things are possible" is not just a nice phrase. It's the door that opens every opportunity you are seeking. It's not a magic wand; it's the sword of truth. And that's all you need to accomplish your dreams.

The "wizard" you're seeking is not in Oz but within you where God graciously put a measure of Himself, waiting for you to desire His counsel and direction. Seek Him with your whole heart and you will find Him.

Father in heaven, I suspect I'm as guilty of magical thinking as anyone. Sometimes I hope for things I've neglected to pray about. I wish for things without putting any foundation under my dreams. Help me to seek You first and to look for Your help with all the possibilities that may be ahead. Amen.

51

Possibility Procrastinator

And let us not grow weary while doing good, for in
due season we shall reap if we do not lose heart.
GALATIANS 6:9 NKJV

f you've identified some particular idea, goal, or hobby you'd like to do that may catapult you into what's still possible, what keeps you from going after it? Chances are good that the possibility procrastinator steps in. It may not shoot down your ideas like a science-fiction Terminator, but it sidetracks you just the same.

Maybe you tell a friend about your idea, and they burst your balloon of hope. They talk about the downsides so much that you start wondering why you wanted to do it in the first place. Sometimes you keep your idea on the back burner, immerse yourself in work, and get so buried you don't have time to put your possibility into play. You'll rationalize that immediate work is more important than future dreams.

The closer you get to making a move toward what is possible, you sabotage yourself so you simply can't find a minute to take a single step forward. You might even go out of your way to invent things you have to do, like cleaning the garage or sorting through your last three thousand emails.

If you'd like to avoid some of these missteps to your future, try stopping everything and taking it all to God. Ask Him to create new possibilities. Ask Him to spur you on so you don't delay the process out of fear that it might not work . . . or that it will. God makes things possible, but He can do it best if you're not putting everything on hold, ignoring His little nudges, or hiding behind your fears.

Finding ways to procrastinate is a very human trait and one that might need your honest attention. If you're truly ready to move forward to your next awesome possibility, then find your balloon, fill it with inspiration, and let it soar. You will be glad you did!

Lord, thank You for the gift of inspired ideas to pursue as I look at what may still be possible in the next few years. Help me not to procrastinate when I can take action on my dreams now. Whatever You and I find to do, Lord, I pray it will be a blessing to others. Amen.

52

Let's Play "What If?"

For what if some did not believe? Will their unbelief
make the faithfulness of God without effect?
ROMANS 3:3 NKJV

The game of "what if?" is an interesting one because our first inclination is to give it a negative spin. As we consider a new opportunity, a new relationship, or even a deeper commitment to God, we play the game as though we need to consider all the possibilities that might go wrong. We say, "What if I take this job promotion and discover I'm not able to handle it?" Or, "What if I invest in this new relationship more than the other person invests in me?" Or, "What if I tell God I will go wherever He wants me to go and He sends me to work outside my comfort zone?" *What if?* can be a bit scary.

However, you can also use the "what if?" game to imagine the best. When you do, you might stumble onto amazing possibilities for your life. You might say, "What if I accept the promotion and I discover it suits me perfectly?" Or, "What if I invest in the relationship and it works out even better than I can imagine?" Or, "What if I tell God I will go wherever He wants me to go, and

He sends me to the people and the places I have been longing for my whole life?"

The Bible tells us to seek first the kingdom of God. When you do—when you desire to know those things that are righteous before God—He will act on your behalf. He will add blessing after blessing to your life.

As you look forward to discovering what God has for you, skip the "what if?" question and start by asking God directly what He would have you do instead. Show Him you want to please Him above all else, and He will bless you in His perfect timing.

The God of all things sees you and knows the desires of your heart. He knows the right work for you to do and the right relationships for you to invest in. He always has a new possibility for you to explore. Set your intention with Him and He will bless the work of your hands and heart.

Lord of All, help me to seek Your face before I make any big decisions in my life. Remind me to put all my possibilities at Your feet and only choose the ones that You have designed for me. Amen.

53

The Possibility Eight Ball

Would not God search this out? For He
knows the secrets of the heart.

PSALM 44:21 NKJV

No doubt, you've had a Magic 8-Ball experience in life. Not the kind you sink into the side pocket of the billiard table but the little black ball that tells your future by answering yes or no questions. When you were a kid, you may have been duped into believing it had some magical powers, but the magic probably disappeared as the Magic 8-Ball just repeated yes, no, and maybe over and over. It wasn't a mysterious oracle after all.

Though we may laugh at the Magic 8-Ball idea, consider those times when you are indecisive and fall back on eight-ball questions. The "yes, no, and maybe" construct limits you from digging deep enough to get real answers. Yes and no questions seldom show all possibilities.

So, what's different about asking God questions? God is real, and He sees your heart. He knows what motivates your questions, and He has the best answers. His answers go way past yes and no. Sure, you can ask if this is the right time to move to a new city, but it's likely God won't send an email with a big *yes* on it. He will put things into position to make it easy for you to move. He will open doors to the right job and the right location for your new home. He will give you a response that lets you know He's with you.

When you seek God's direction for the things that are still possible for you to accomplish, watch what happens around and within you. A friend may call out of the blue with a part of the answer. You may see an ad for the exact solution to your problem. Solutions you never expected will start to come together, and the answer will be clear.

These aren't coincidences; this is God's answer to your prayers. You can depend on God to keep you in His grace and mercy so you will never be behind the eight ball in life.

Lord, thank You for showing up for me and helping me understand Your direction for my life. Give me wisdom to wait for You and to look for Your answers anytime I come to You with questions. I praise Your name today. Amen.

54

Widening the Net

And let us consider how we may spur one
another on toward love and good deeds.
HEBREWS 10:24

ost of us need encouragement to try new things. After all, widening the net of our possibilities can be a bit scary. It's been said that encouragement is oxygen for your soul and most new ventures require you to take a deep breath before you jump in. So, where do you go for the right kind of encouragement?

Let's start with the usual suspects. You confide in your spouse, sharing your thoughts on going back to school to get an advanced degree and your feeling of excitement about diving into a new course of study. Your spouse reminds you that it's expensive to get an advanced degree and that you'll have to compete with much younger candidates for the same jobs. *Pop!* There goes one of your balloons.

So you decide to share your dream with a close-friend, and she just laughs out loud that you can't be serious. When your friend realizes you are, in fact, serious, she listens with awe and says how amazing you are, unable to actually give you thoughts on moving forward because she thinks it's a crazy idea. You are deflated once again.

Okay, so you've tried to get encouragement from your spouse and your friend, and you have come up empty. What's next?

Go to Jesus, the Great Fisherman! When Jesus called His disciples, He was looking for one key response. He didn't seek the ones who had to go home and check with a family member or a friend to see if they should consider following Him; He looked for the ones who jumped in when He cast the net of possibility in front of them. He looked for those who were ready to move at His call.

Perhaps today is a good day to seek His calling on your life. If the desires of your heart are part of His plan for you, you can be sure He will widen the net and the doors will open to make your dreams possible. He's ready to encourage every step you take. The funny thing is that once you take steps toward your dreams, others will come alongside you to encourage you to keep going forward.

Father God, I am so grateful You know my heart and my desires to keep growing and moving forward in my life. I want to be all I can to bring honor to You and fulfill my purpose here on earth. I pray You will open doors to those opportunities that are meant for me. Amen.

55

The Eye of the Needle

"Again I tell you, it is easier for a camel to go through the eye of a needle than for someone who is rich to enter the kingdom of God."

MATTHEW 19:24

S cholars may debate Jesus' intention with this illustration from Matthew, but if you read the whole passage, you'll see that a rich young ruler in the story was a good man who had been humble and giving. The problem was he wasn't quite ready to give up *everything* he had to follow Jesus.

So what is your "eye of the needle," that thing you can't quite give up to surrender your whole heart to God? Figuring out what is still possible for you may hinge on those things you aren't quite willing to give up, or at least to give over to God's care and keeping.

The rich young ruler wanted to know what else he needed to do to follow Jesus, but he was disappointed when he heard the answer. What about us? We may imagine we have already done the things that Jesus would require. We've given to others, applied our hearts to charity, and attended church on a regular basis. As far as we can tell, we've been model citizens. So what stops us from taking that one last step to make a full commitment?

We don't know if the young ruler ever decided to do what Jesus requested, but we know we can decide. We can choose to follow Him so He can lead us into even more amazing possibilities, or we can choose to hold on to what we've got. We might have our own heroic stories, our own prize trophies that we're not willing to risk. After all, we've done enough.

Ah, there's the rub! Who defines what is enough? Recall the poor widow who put two mites into the collection box. She was considered extremely generous because she gave everything she had to God. She didn't hold anything back.

The beauty of an open hand is that it most often is accompanied by an open heart. When we want God to give generously to us, we have to make sure we don't hold anything back from Him. With an open hand and an open heart, we find the way to all that is still possible.

Lord of the Possible, remind me to always be prepared to give up anything You've given me in favor of Your blessing and Your direction. Only You know my whole story and what You've planned for me to do next. I praise Your name! Amen.

56

Get Ready! Get Set! Go!

This is the one about whom it is written: "I will send my
messenger ahead of you, who will prepare your way before you."

MATTHEW 11:10

hat does it mean to "get ready" to move into a new way
of thinking or a new opportunity? Getting ready is about
praying fervently for God's help. It's about figuring out what
you'd like to do. You spend time talking to friends, doing Internet
searches, and figuring out what piques your interest. Getting
ready is key to moving forward.

Once you're ready, it's time to get set. When you're set, it
means you know exactly what you're going after. You don't doubt
yourself, question your possibilities, or wonder whether to try or
not try. You're set. You are laser focused, and you know the target.
You've put it all in God's hands, and you know you're ready when
opportunity knocks. It's significant.

When God sees that you are set, He determines the timing,
the moment, the precise measure of all things that will make your
hopes possible. It's a nuclear moment when all the right things

collide and explode into the most glorious possibility you've ever had. All engines are set to go.

God has incredible plans for you. When He knows you're prepared to go forward, He says, "Ready, set, go!"

Nothing is too big or too small to keep you from moving forward. You and God together are an incredible force for good. Praise God for all that is possible for you now.

Lord, I pray You will help me to set the direction for all You mean for me. Keep me moving, Lord, as I wait for Your signal to go! Help me not get in the way of all You want me to do. Amen.

57

The Possibility Box

All the officers and people were happy to bring their money,
and they put it in the box until the box was full.

2 CHRONICLES 24:10 NCV

ost of us focus on the present with an eye on the future. We are planners, and we encourage future possibilities by saving our money for that proverbial rainy day. We do it because we believe somewhere up ahead an opportunity will present itself, and we want to be ready to embrace it.

The Israelites were on that same track. They were pooling their resources so they could prepare for an event yet to come. They were creating a possibility box. If you haven't been able to set aside funds for your future, there may be other ways you can gather resources for new opportunities to create your own possibility box too.

Of course, the first step is to make deposits into your spiritual bank account. The more you invest your time with the Source of All That's Possible, the more you can bank on building future assets. God's blessings are infinite, and they will continue to flow into your life at every age and stage.

Give yourself permission to imagine the things God could do with your gifts and talents. Make a list of the ways you've been personally equipped to manage life, encourage others, or cause people to smile. As you look at those things, focus on them so that they become bigger. As you consider those options, make a note and slip them into your possibility box. Ask your friends what makes you special. Let them also make deposits into your possibility box.

Now you are ready to go back to the bank. Your box is full of possible directions. You can deposit those into a safe place, and God will protect those ideas and provide opportunities as He chooses.

Saving for a rainy day isn't always easy. Putting possibilities in a box and hoping they might come to fruition is even more difficult. You can be assured that God has been investing in you and waiting for the perfect time to give you a new possibility. He's ready when you are!

Dear Lord, thank You for investing in my future and for knowing the perfect time for me to embrace a new direction and purpose. I pray that I will be open to Your call and will please You with the work I do. Amen.

58

What Dreamers Know

*He said, "Listen to my words: When prophets are
among you, I, the LORD, will show myself to them
in visions; I will speak to them in dreams."*

NUMBERS 12:6 NCV

erhaps when you were growing up, you were labeled a
dreamer. You let your mind wander as you imagined all
that was possible in the world around you. You saw things differently from those who were focused on daily routines. The adage
"All who wander, aren't necessarily lost" may apply to you.

Of course, in the days of the prophets, God shared things in
visions and dreams with the ones who spoke in His name. He
communicated with them in ways that were real and powerful.

Though your dreams are not quite in that league, your willingness to wonder, imagining the use of your skills and talents
in new ways, may have been given to you by God. He wants to
honor those gifts He inspired within you.

William James wrote, "Most people never run far enough on
their first wind to find out they've got a second. Give your dreams
all you've got, and you'll be amazed at the energy that comes out

of you." If you're looking forward to getting a "second wind," tap into the dreams you're carrying in your heart and mind. There may be some vision there, some glimpse of possibility that is ready to come to fruition. Then submit your dreams to God and seek the way He would have you go. He has the path well marked so that you can win the day.

Proverbs 29:18 reminds us that without vision, the people perish. On the other hand, it is reasonable to believe that, when we have a vision inspired by God's grace and kindness, we can expect to thrive and find fulfillment. Go after your dreams today!

Lord of All Dreams, Your Spirit inspired the prophets of old and the dreams of people over the centuries. You have been continually creating new hope and possibility in our hearts and minds. Help me receive Your gifts today that will inspire my direction tomorrow. Amen.

59

Just Show Up!

God, order up your power; show the mighty
power you have used for us before.
PSALM 68:28 NCV

God is the same yesterday, today, and forever. He is the same in power and glory and mercy and love. He is the same in faithfulness and steadfast generosity. He never leaves us desolate or alone. He never condemns us to a place where forgiveness is not possible. He sees you right where you are, and He will show up when you ask Him to draw near. That's a promise.

Can you remember those times when God showed up for you? If so, then you have a great place to start as you seek His face for your future, for the things you still hope are possible. Your energy, your resources, and your patience may all run low, but your Father in heaven has unlimited resources. He offers you the power of the Godhead, the three-in-one mystery, to help you at any time. God the Father, God the Son, and God the Holy Spirit will show up for you when you call for His direction, help, and blessings.

Norman Vincent Peale wrote, "One of the most powerful

concepts, one which is a sure cure for lack of confidence, is the thought that God is with you and helping you. This is one of the simplest teachings in religion, namely, that Almighty God will be your companion, will stand by you, help you, and see you through. No other idea is so powerful in developing self-confidence as this simple belief when practiced. To practice it simply affirm, 'God is with me; God is helping me; God is guiding me.' Spend several minutes each day visualizing His presence. Then practice believing that affirmation."

It appears God's power is limited only by our lack of belief. Make it your practice to remind yourself God is with you and He guides you to those places and people that will make a difference, helping you define all that is still possible for you.

Lord God, thank You for love that goes beyond my ability to comprehend it. Help me to trust You so much that I walk confidently forward, believing in all that You have yet designed for me to accomplish. Amen.

60

Where the Possibility Ends

*"Teach them to obey everything that I have taught you, and
I will be with you always, even until the end of this age."*

MATTHEW 28:20 NCV

ou may have imagined that you can run out of possibilities
in life. You might even think that you've made too many
haphazard decisions and that God is simply done with you. After
all, what have you done for Him lately? But you are not the reason
all things are possible. God is the reason all things are possible,
and as long as God reigns, possibility never ends.

Jesus wanted His disciples to tell His story. He promised that
if they would teach others about Him, He would always be with
them, even when it might appear that they're at the end of all
possibility.

God gave you free will. He wanted you to know the difference between choosing to live in His presence and choosing to
walk all on your own. God wanted you to experience all that is
possible for you.

C. S. Lewis said, "Why did God give them free will? Because
free will, though it makes evil possible, is also the only thing that

makes possible any love or goodness or joy worth having." As you walk more closely with God, lean on His teachings so you see more of all that He wants for you. You have the freedom to choose Him every day and to offer Him all that you are and all you hope to be. When you lean on Him, your possibility never ends.

Lord of All That Is Possible, help me desire to walk with You with my whole heart so that I can serve You and embrace those things that You have made possible. I praise and thank You for giving me free will, and, beyond that, the will to choose You every day. Amen.

61

You've Got This!

*But one thing I do, forgetting those things which are behind
and reaching forward to those things which are ahead.*

PHILIPPIANS 3:13 NKJV

When you look forward to new possibilities, you may start with a review of your past. You may look at things you regret, choices that grieve your spirit, and unresolved emotions that drift through your mind. Upon reflection, you wonder why God even puts up with you.

The first thing to recognize is God never "puts up" with you. God's love for you is so great that no amount of your foolishness will keep Him away from you. He may be sad when you walk ahead of Him or when you don't talk to Him, but it's because He knows how much you need Him.

Those unwise choices you've already prayed about have been forgiven . . . and forgotten! God is not making a chart of your sins so He can remind you of them. Every sin you have confessed has been forgiven. The past is passed. God wants you to stop looking back. Instead, reach forward, upward, and outward so that He can move you toward things He wants for you now.

As you lean in to listen to God's voice, He gently reminds you that "You've got this!" You can take on the future because He is right there beside you. He has extraordinary plans for your life, and He is excited that you are ready to embrace those plans. He creates new possibilities for you with every sunrise, and nothing makes Him happier than sharing those plans with you.

Don't spend one more moment looking back. Just look up to the heavens, to the One who waits to give you more of what He has already planned. He knows you can do it. You've got this!

Lord God, thank You for Your immeasurable love and Your continual forgiveness. Give me a clean heart, ready to take on the future with joy. Thank You for shining Your light on my possibilities. Amen.

62

The Spirit of Possibility

*To do this, I work and struggle, using Christ's great
strength that works so powerfully in me.*

COLOSSIANS 1:29 NCV

Believing in the idea of possibility means you believe you
have options, prospects, and opportunities ahead. That
spirit of possibility is shaped by your core beliefs. What you
imagine to be possible drives you forward.

Sometimes you have so much faith you actually imagine getting a mountain to move from its spot. At other times, you don't
have enough faith to order your lunch. Checking in with your
spirit and seeing how closely it is aligned with God's Spirit may
give you a better understanding.

God's Spirit is all-powerful. It has no end and it never grows
weary. It is so powerful it can create worlds out of nothing and
human beings out of dust. Humans are too finite to fully understand the force God actually is. He gives us as much of His Spirit
as we can stand, knowing His power would consume us if He
drew too near. You may recall how God protected Moses when
He chose to speak to him directly. He didn't want to get too close.

That same power of God, then, exists in Christ who is God. It exists in some portion in our hearts. It grows more powerful as our faith is able to sustain it. God is our power, the true wind beneath our wings.

Imagine that the Spirit of All Possibility is drawing close to you. He is longing to give you more than you have now because you have important things to accomplish. If you can imagine that, perhaps you can embrace His Spirit more fully, clinging to it, so you can recognize each door He opens on your behalf.

When your heart is full of the Spirit of Possibility, amazing things are up ahead. Believe in all God has done and share His stories, and He will create new opportunities for you. Thank Him for all He is doing right now in your life.

Lord, I do not always recognize Your power or Your infinite ability to do amazing things. Help me to seek more of You so I can draw on Your incredible Spirit for new options and blessings. Amen.

63

Pumping Up Your Possibilities

Make every effort to keep the unity of the
Spirit through the bond of peace.
EPHESIANS 4:3

Think about a balloon. It's designed to fly. It has incredible possibilities to float high and travel far. It's colorful and brilliant, and yet, no matter how well or how beautifully designed it is, it can't go anywhere without air. It needs to be pumped up and filled before it can do all that it was meant to do.

You, also, were skillfully and lovingly created. You were designed for a purpose, meant to become something amazing. If you're still on the ground, still trying to figure out how to get a little further, it might be time to see what's missing, what you need to pump you up. No doubt you need air!

The Spirit of God is the breath of life, the Source of your possibility, the Inspiration for your soul. God knows how to fill you and how to help you soar in the things you do, and He is ready at any time to reward your efforts as you seek to know more of Him.

One of the best things you can do is become more lighthearted, seeking to align yourself with God's will and purpose. When you do, His peace will fill your soul and set your mind at ease. The more you understand God's plans for your life, the better, brighter, warmer, and lighter you will feel. When you trust all that God has for you, you are free to soar.

If you feel lifeless, barely able to navigate the world around you, and in need of new direction, go to God in prayer. Ask Him to pump you up with possibility and joy. Ask Him to blow fresh breezes into your life so you can rise and shine again. When you are filled with God's love, you are inspired and free to lift your voice high in praise and give glory to your Father in heaven.

Lord, thank You for being my Source of inspiration and for filling me up when I am deflated, feeling undervalued and overwhelmed. Help me look to You for peace of mind so I can move forward with a light heart to serve You. Amen.

64

When the Well Runs Dry

But you should be strong. Don't give up, because
you will get a reward for your good work.
2 CHRONICLES 15:7 NCV

When the patriarchs traveled across the lands God gave them and settled their new lives in Canaan, they would have dug several wells. They knew a desert city could not be built without a source of water. Ancient wells first appeared over 8,500 years ago. You may recall the story of Jacob's well, the place where Jesus met the Samaritan woman and gave her Living Water.

We may not depend on well water these days, but we appreciate the symbol of hope and possibility wells brought to those early nomadic tribes. When the well ran dry, they had to move on and find a new source of water.

The well is a good metaphor for faith. When we want to settle down, create roots, and begin new things, we dig in. We dig into the surrounding possibilities and look for the best opportunities. We flourish for a while, but when life takes a downturn or grows stagnant, we feel choked by weeds of doubt. We wonder if it's time to quit and move on.

The answer is in where you've dug the well. If you have immersed yourself in Living Water, you can go to the Source and seek new direction. Looking deeply into the well, you see all God has done to reward your efforts and sustain your life.

The well of Living Water never runs dry. Jesus fills you with peace and sends you out into the world, refreshed and renewed every time you turn to Him.

A desert well sustains those who drink from it, but it may eventually run dry. The water from the well of God's love and blessing will sustain you for a lifetime. Come to His well every day, and allow the love of Christ to renew and refresh you with His never-ending cup of possibility and joy.

Lord, it's not always easy to keep moving forward, seeking new ideas and possibilities. Sometimes I simply want to give up. Please fill me with Your Living Water so I can be sustained from here to eternity. I pray to dig my roots deeply into Your divine resources. Amen.

65

Once Upon a Time

Day after day they tell the story; night after night they tell it again.

PSALM 19:2 NCV

A golden cliché of storytelling is the opening phrase "once upon a time." It has origins going back to the 1300s and has been used in dozens of cultures and languages. It communicates a beginning without defining a particular time in history. As children, we were always drawn in by the expectation of great fantasy and adventure when a story began with those four words.

Storytelling was also God's way of getting the word out about Himself. He reminded His children often how important it was for them to share the things He had done. Why? Because each generation had to frame the divine nature of God for those who came after them. They had to know God was real.

Imagine what your life would be like if no one had ever told you the story of God's saving grace and love. As you've seen before, history is really His story: God's legacy and the place we return to refresh our hearts and minds. Without the story, nothing is possible.

The better you know God, the more you can tell detailed and

loving stories about Him. You're an ambassador of His love and helping to build His legacy.

Such storytelling does not depend on how well you tell the story but about the enthusiasm and spirit with which you tell it. The more connected you are to the story itself, the more real it will feel to those who are listening. You add the drama of a miraculous moment. You send shivers up the spine of those who never knew God could show up in such a fantastic way. You bring God's immeasurable possibilities to life.

Billy Graham wrote that your life may be the only Bible some people will ever read. When you begin to tell His tales, you may well start with "once upon a time," but you will continue on into "happily ever after." It's God's story and you can tell it well. After all, it's the only story of possibility that really exists.

Author of Us All, help me to tell Your story with passion and joy so others want to know what happens next, so they draw closer to You each day. Because of Your story, I have opportunities and possibilities to look forward to discovering each day. Amen.

66

Own the Zone

Each person must be responsible for himself.
GALATIANS 6:5 NCV

As parents, we strive to raise children who are self-reliant and self-confident. We want them to demonstrate self-control so they are responsible human beings who care about others and admit when they are wrong. But even as adults, it's difficult to own the zone, the area in which we contributed to chaos or harm.

We want to honor positive attributes, but we don't usually succeed all by ourselves. It's easy to own our actions when we feel good about a great accomplishment. It's much harder when things have fallen apart and we recognize that we had a hand in a negative outcome.

Part of chasing possibilities in life is taking the responsibility to assess your ownership of your actions. It's not about casting stones at your failures but about owning responsibility and then moving on. Moving on may mean you have a mess to clean up, but once you do, something good can follow and you'll be back on track. You own the cleanup and you own the positive outcome. God wants you to find joy in the work of your hands, but you should confess anything that deflates your best intentions to Him.

Owning the zone means not making excuses for things that didn't go well for you. It means you're walking with God in mercy and love and realizing that without His forgiveness, you wouldn't get anywhere. It means you acknowledge you made poor choices and you are accepting blame as easily as you accept kudos.

Take some time to sort through your old scrapbooks or your camera roll from years ago, and look at those old moments with new eyes. Ask yourself what part you played in the outcome that gives you greater possibilities today. You may be surprised to see the ways God has been leading you. After all, He knows you very well.

Lord, I don't always like having to own my actions. I realize now, Lord, that I've always been in control of my choices and I own the things I have done for good and for harm. I ask for Your forgiveness and Your guidance as I seek new possibilities for the future. Amen.

67

God's Great Plans

Eye has not seen, nor ear heard, nor have entered into the heart of man the things which God has prepared for those who love Him.

1 CORINTHIANS 2:9 NKJV

As you seek new possibilities, how big are you willing to go? Oh sure, you can find nice things to do that won't cause you to grow or change in any way. You can settle for one more low-hanging fruit of opportunity and call it good. The question, though, is "Why?" Why would you look for new direction and only make plans for the mediocre?

If you've taken your hopes and dreams to God, did you do your best to convince Him to give you one little tiny cup of blessing? Did you feel like a beggar going to the well and hoping you would somehow be able to get a drink?

If those questions resonate with you, look back at 1 Corinthians 2:9. This verse describes God's plans for you, the plans He made for all the people who love Him. It says you have never seen or heard anything that compares to what God has prepared for you. You can search the Internet all you want; you will not find the equivalent of anything the Designer has planned. It's

136

so big, God challenges you to try to imagine it. It's POSSIBILITY in capital letters. You can look for it, but you won't get a glimpse because even your heart is blind to what God has in mind.

What are you willing to imagine? You cast your bread on the waters and open yourself to the possibility that amazing things could come floating back to you. God sees you and loves you and He's already planning awesome surprises for your future. He is a big God, a gracious God, and open to giving you bigger opportunities right now. You might find a gallon jug or maybe a water tower to fill at the well instead of that little cup.

Father in heaven, it inspires my heart to imagine the things You've planned for the people who love you. Help me come to You and be open to greater fulfillment of my heart's desires. Help me to trust in You, Lord, for all that is still possible. Amen.

68

Seven Uses for Peanut Butter

Tell them not to spend their time on stories that are not true and
on long lists of names in family histories. These things only bring
arguments; they do not help God's work, which is done in faith.

1 TIMOTHY 1:4 NCV

It's satisfying to create a list of chores or activities and systematically cross them out as you complete each task. It makes you feel productive and helps to organize your thoughts. It also helps you get results.

In that same spirit, you might try to create a possibilities list. Brainstorm every possible avenue you could explore to add dimension to your life. For practice, consider ways to use leftover chicken or the last cup of peanut butter. You may discover that until you actually focus your efforts on one specific topic, you get stuck in your old habits. You have to give yourself permission to go beyond your usual boundaries to get new combinations of ideas. How else will you know that peanut butter is an excellent topping for carrots?

A list gives you things to focus on until you get the job done. When you want to move into a new life direction, make a list.

Take your ideas to God, then sit down and write down the potential directions you could go. Pray over the list and see if anything stands out. Name people or places that might help you move forward. The main thing is to keep the list positive and play with ideas. Pick a possibility topic and imagine every new way to create it. You may invent seven new uses for peanut butter.

Once you feel you've exhausted your ideas, go back to God and ask for guidance about what to pursue first. He's sure to help you set a few priorities to move things along. Who knows, you may become the peanut butter expert!

Lord God, I understand why making a list is helpful. After all, You created the entire world in an orderly way and set a priority for each day. Help me to focus on ways to create new possibilities for my life and come to You with my list of ideas. I give You thanks and praise. Amen.

69

Getting a Face-Lift

A happy heart makes the face cheerful,
but heartache crushes the spirit.
PROVERBS 15:13

f you buy into the idea that "we're never truly dressed without
a smile," then you understand that having a cheerful heart
has nothing to do with your outfit. It has everything to do with
how you outfit your heart and mind. In other words, what's going
on within you can either crush your spirit or cause your face to
shine. If you feel a need for a face-lift, don't start at the mirror;
start with prayer.

When your spirit is crushed, nothing feels possible. It's hard
to pray. It's hard to imagine God is near. Probably nothing shows
up more readily on your face than heartache.

In 1 Samuel 16:7 we read that "people look at the outward
appearance, but the LORD looks at the heart." Perhaps then, we
need to step away from those things that have caused us grief or
misunderstanding and grasp the heart of the matter. Our hearts
are designed to carry the light of God's love. When we see Him

with the eyes of our hearts, we begin to comprehend that He is with us always, in good times and difficult ones.

You may feel nothing is possible for you today, but that isn't how God feels. He sees you. He knows you need this time to be reflective and thoughtful. He waits for you to be ready to move on again.

Your job then is to be willing to exchange the heartache for the heart delight that God has already prepared. When you're ready to reach up, to see beyond all that exists in your current circumstances, you'll be ready for a face-lift. As you think of your future possibilities, remember God is with you now and goes ahead of you into the future. The cloudy days will pass and give way to the amazing beauty of all He has yet planned for you. He holds every possibility for you in His heart. Go to Him and you will find the way.

Lord, on days when I cannot even *imagine* a good thing happening, I know I'm having the worst kind of heart trouble. I ask to feel Your presence and be willing to surrender all that holds me back from the joy You want me to experience. Help me to keep believing in Your possibilities for me. Amen.

70

Your Top Ten

He declared to you his covenant, the Ten Commandments, which he commanded you to follow and then wrote them on two stone tablets.

DEUTERONOMY 4:13

Our culture loves top ten lists. We like to know the top ten podcasts, or the best-selling books, or the top ten websites on our favorite topics. We feel on top of what's happening because we just like knowing things.

In some measure, when God offered the Ten Commandments to the people of Israel, He was trying to help them answer their questions about how to live the best life. What should they focus on? How should they set priorities? As it turns out, the Ten Commandments are as valuable for us today as they were when Moses carried them down from the mountain.

As you seek God's direction and favor, consider making your own top ten and setting goals that align with the desires of your heart. Your possibility list might coincide with the list Moses presented to Israel, because you would start out the same way—heart first, seeking the Lord and loving Him above all else. Focus on all the ways you can please Him and keep Him a priority.

After that, you might look at ways to bring honor to your home and your family, your parents and your children. Opportunities that offer respect for people you love would be worth pursuing. Seek to be above board in all your dealings, striving to do those things that please God. Be a giver and not a taker, seeking possibilities that allow you to be generous in your heart, mind, and soul.

When your intention is to serve God better, He will go ahead of you, opening doors and guiding your steps. Keep Him number one and you may find your best possibilities are off the charts!

Lord God, help me keep You at the beginning of my top ten list, no matter what I am trying to accomplish. I believe in You with my whole heart, and I trust that You always know the way to keep me moving forward. I praise Your name! Amen.

71

What a Masterpiece!

For we are God's masterpiece. He has created us anew in Christ
Jesus, so we can do the good things he planned for us long ago.
EPHESIANS 2:10 NLT

God may not have needed a blueprint or a rough draft to wind up with a masterpiece, but we do. We need a fresh canvas, a vision, or a great idea before we can create anything new or even if we want to polish up an old idea. It's just not in our skill set to be able to create something out of nothing. We have to surround ourselves with plans and ideas, wads of paper that represent discarded attempts and stories and photos of inspiration. If things go well, we will stumble onto our masterpiece and it will be as much of a surprise to us as it is to anyone else.

The writer of Ephesians suggests that once Jesus entered the earth's arena, He brought a bright new canvas, a clean slate, and a finished manuscript. He made it possible for us to do the good things God planned long ago. With the help of Jesus, we not only become a useful piece of art but something even more extraordinary: a masterpiece of incredible design. If we accept that information and take it to heart, it is up to us to determine how we will showcase God's work in us.

Imagine that Jesus has handed you a clean slate of your life and has instructed you to create a masterpiece, something only you can do. He promises He'll be right there with you and that you will definitely succeed. He will never leave your side. All you have to do is trust Him and believe that all things are possible through Him.

Erase the limitations you've imposed on yourself and you will see things you've never considered possible before. You'll go after the rest of your life with gusto knowing that, with God at your side, you can't help but create a masterpiece.

Go then! Here's a new canvas! Become the masterpiece God designed you to be. Your possibilities are endless!

Creator God, I pray I will put every potential opportunity I have into Your capable hands. I ask that You return to me those things that I am truly designed to do. Help me to be a living work of art for You! Amen.

72

What Profits You?

Plant your seed in the morning and keep busy all
afternoon, for you don't know if profit will come
from one activity or another—or maybe both.

ECCLESIASTES 11:6 NLT

Though we may think of money when we hear the word *profit*, it may not be the most appropriate definition. What profits us are those things that work for our good. What profits you may look quite different from what profits someone else.

Solomon offered guidance about how we might discover our possibilities. He suggested we plant seeds in the morning. Apart from that four-foot square of earth where you're able to grow tomatoes in each summer, how else can you plant seeds?

You can plant seeds of gratitude, thanking God for all you have right now. Focus on those things you may take for granted like your comfortable bed, a warm shower, or a hearty breakfast. Reflect on things that help you see the world in a positive light so you notice how God has blessed the seeds you planted in the past.

Once you're prepared for the day, plant more seeds by spending time with people you love, sending notes to those who cross your mind in prayer, and lending a helping hand to those who are near you. The seeds of kindness always profit you because the good you do for others comes back to you tenfold.

Before you know it, the morning is spent, but the verse says it's best to stay busy all afternoon as well. Why? Because you don't know when good seeds will sprout. Each seed is a possibility. You may enjoy the reward from one idea more than another, or you may profit from them equally, but what matters is your effort. You were intentional about creating something new.

Any effort on your part brings joy to God's heart. Seeds you planted before still generate great possibilities. Remind yourself that with God all things may become seeds of greatness and what's still possible for you is simply glorious.

Lord of the Harvest, I am busy planting seeds, preparing the soil, and getting ready for all that is to come. Bless my efforts and allow new opportunities to take root and bloom. I come to You with a heart of gratitude for the amazing things You've already done in my life. You bring me delight with each sunrise. Amen.

73

Deep Knee Bends

Always be joyful. Never stop praying. Be
thankful in all circumstances, for this is God's
will for you who belong to Christ Jesus.
1 THESSALONIANS 5:16–18 NLT

oing deep knee bends may not be quite as easy as it used to be. After all, your knees are older than they once were. Bending may now cause you to groan a bit, so you prefer to say your prayers from a comfortable chair rather than the floor.

When you think about it, you're a pretty amazing design. After all, if God hadn't created you exactly as you are, bending may not have been possible. He knit you together in your mother's womb so you could be flexible, able to bend without breaking. When you choose to go to your knees in prayer, you humble yourself before Him, and He knows you are fully committed to sharing those things that concern you. He sees you on your knees, and He lifts you up, bringing you closer to Him.

Thank God for all He did to design you so perfectly. He gave you people to care for you, nurture you, and help you get on your feet. He gave you laughter and tears and the ability to feel joy and wonder and disappointment. He made happiness possible for you.

You may not know what is still possible for you, but the One who has known you since before your birth has more possibilities available to you. He shaped and molded your thinking, talents, and skills of every kind so you would be ready for this moment in time.

Think of how often He bends down to be near to you, bends to forgive you, and bends to straighten the path you walk. Let Him know today that you trust Him with every moment of your life. Trust is the deepest kind of knee-bending you can offer God. Trust is what allows Him to move closer to you to make more things possible.

Father in heaven, I bend to Your will, surrendering my heart to You and seeking Your direction for all that I might yet be. Help me to remember You have been with me from the beginning of my days. I yield to Your generous plans for my future. Amen.

149

74

Piecrust Promises

*A person who promises a gift but doesn't give it is
like clouds and wind that bring no rain.*

PROVERBS 25:14 NLT

In the original *Mary Poppins* film, upon hearing a child make a promise, Mary Poppins says, "Those are piecrust promises; easily made and easily broken." Her sentiment rings a bell to those of us who often too easily make promises that are too easily broken. Why is it so hard to keep a promise?

A promise is only as good as the person who makes it. When a person promises a gift or makes a commitment but then doesn't follow through, it's like seeing the clouds but getting no rain. Sadly, we make commitments but find reasons not to honor them. Of course, at times we have no choice but to break a promise, but our hope is to realize that every promise is important.

Promises kept build trust and relationships. This is the way you learned about trusting God too. The Bible assures you God keeps His promises. He promises to be with you all through life, and He will be. He promises that all things are possible through Him and that He can do great things through you. He never makes a piecrust promise. He never says one thing and does another. He's a promise keeper.

Since God has set the standard for keeping promises, the best thing we can do is emulate Him. We can strive only to promise things we can deliver. Standard business practice may revolve around over-promising and under-delivering, but that is not God's practice.

As God walks with you today, thank Him for past promises where He showed up and delivered a perfect solution or a new possibility. He has earned your trust, so you know that with Him alone you can find all that is possible for your life.

Lord, I am always awed at Your faithfulness. You stick by me when others leave. You forgive my impulsive piecrust promises. You cause me to want to be a better person with each new day. Amen.

75

That's a Crazy Idea!

You are bringing some strange ideas to our ears,
and we would like to know what they mean.

ACTS 17:20

You've probably had a few crazy ideas in your life; you know, the kind no one can understand because the idea just doesn't seem reasonable to people who know you. Perhaps you decided to quit your job and move to another country so you could experience a new culture. Perhaps you decided you'd adopt a child after you just celebrated your fiftieth birthday. It's likely that some of the things you want to do with the rest of your life seem a bit crazy to others.

You might say that when God sent a baby boy, His only Son, to be born in a manger in Bethlehem, that was a crazy idea. After all, the Savior of the world would be born to humble parents, He'd have to be a scholar of Scripture, and He'd have to be willing to die for His people. What a strange set of conditions for someone who was meant to be a king! In fact, for some people, the whole idea of God is a bit crazy. "What do you mean there is only one God? What do you mean that this God knows me? Is it true I only have to believe in Him to go to heaven? Isn't that too easy? That sounds crazy!"

When the disciples who traveled with Jesus during His earthly life began to spread the good news about Him and share the story of His birth, death, and resurrection, it sounded impossible, unbelievable, crazy! People who were intrigued, though, leaned in and wanted to know more. They needed more explanation so they could consider the possibilities of the story.

Your ideas, the ones you are considering for the future, may seem impossible to people around you. They may seem a bit crazy. If that's the case, should you abandon those ideas so that others are more comfortable, or should you continue to seek God's face, hear His voice, and stretch your imagination and your faith? You know the One who does the impossible things, and He's on your side.

Keep believing in all that's possible! There's nothing crazy about that!

Lord, thank You for those crazy, over-the-top ideas that cause me to stretch my thinking and step out of my comfort zones. Help me be willing to examine all the possibilities You inspire within me. Thank You for being the Creator of all those crazy, wonderful ideas that are still possible for me. Amen.

76

Give Yourself a Hand

Clap your hands, all you nations; shout to God with cries of joy.

PSALM 47:1

hances are you never take a bow. You do something amazing and, though others might applaud you, you simply take it in stride, telling yourself it was no big thing. It's the humble way to approach little accomplishments. But is it the only way?

What if you not only thanked God and gave the people you work with some high fives, but you gave yourself a hand as well? After all, you followed God's direction, committed your efforts to ultimate success, and realized the joy of doing something wonderful and worthwhile. Give yourself a hand now and then. You can be sure that even if you don't, the angels in heaven are clapping with joy for your humble achievements.

You have to believe in your ability to handle plans before you can execute them well. God is the Master Designer. He knows exactly what you're capable of doing, and He promises to give you only what you can handle. In recognizing what you *can* do, you can imagine what you *might* do. God knows what is possible for you, and He knows how to shape your circumstances. After all, He's a catalyst for change.

So what's ahead for you? What's still possible? Meditate on God's Word and on His presence to discover what He has for you now. The future may be very different than anything you've done before. It may cause you to wonder if you can really do it. That's good! Your weakness is God's strength. Your uncertainty is His opportunity.

Remember, even the guy behind the scenes is asked to come forward and take a bow now and then. After all, the show couldn't go on without him.

Father God, I humbly come before You, grateful that You have given me opportunities to shine. You have caused me to grow and change and deliver outcomes I never imagined were even possible. You have allowed me to get to know who I am in You, and that makes me giddy with happiness. Help me to understand that we're not done yet and that there is more I can do. Amen.

77

As a Matter of Fact

Without weakening in his faith, he faced the fact that his body was as good as dead—since he was about a hundred years old—and that Sarah's womb was also dead.

ROMANS 4:19

We work hard to understand fact over fiction. We want to know what to trust and how to get at the truth. We gather facts as evidence of what is possible.

Abraham knew God could do anything, but him becoming "father of the year" didn't really seem like a possibility. Sarah was on the same page. When the angel said something akin to, "As a matter of fact, Sarah will give birth around this time next year," poor Sarah couldn't help but laugh. It just wasn't possible. She was well beyond the normal childbearing years. The whole idea seemed ridiculous!

So it is with the human mind and experience. We're quick to point out those things we believe to be facts when we're trying to convince people of our argument. We accept that there are certain principles of science and biology that we can do nothing about. The fact is a ninety-year-old woman doesn't usually give birth. Her biological clock stopped ticking a long time ago. The facts don't lie.

Facts may not lie, but they don't always tell the whole story. They don't start with the premise of possibility. They don't consider the will of the One who created the biological clock in the first place. As a matter of fact, He may be changing the rules altogether.

When we're forced to step aside from the facts, we are left with faith. The One who created all that is can change things as He sees fit. He can open empty wombs, revive faded dreams, and make things new again. As a matter of fact, He can create a possibility any time at all.

So what about you? What dream from your past makes you laugh even to consider it today? If you can believe in the fact that all things are possible with God, you may be holding your dreams in your hand even yet. That's a fact!

Lord God, it's difficult for me even to imagine the story of Abraham and Sarah having a baby at such advanced ages. I realize the point of the story is that You can do anything. Help me to believe in Your possibility more than the facts that dismiss the dreams I try hard to forget. Amen.

78

Us and Them

*You probably think the land belongs to the powerful
and only the privileged have a right to it!*

JOB 22:8 NLT

We often lose focus about what is possible because we spend too much time looking at where we are and not enough time looking at where we want to go. For example, if you're from a small town where very little changes and few people ever move on to create notable opportunities, you might think it isn't possible for you to do more than you do. After all, you imagine that where you live could hold you back.

If you went to a big-city high school with several hundred people in your graduating class, and you graduated in the bottom third, you might imagine that you aren't going to go very far in the world. You might quit before you even try because you suppose others have more possibility to succeed. You may not realize that school grades are rarely indicators of success in life.

Think for a moment about the people Jesus invited into His inner circle. Did He look for the people who lived in big houses and had lots of servants? Did He seek out the local celebrities or the president of the yacht club? Jesus went after the people who were hardworking, were diligent about their tasks, and had a heart for others. He looked for those who were willing to be trained and who hoped for greater opportunities. He looked for people like you: intelligent, caring, and capable. More than that, He wanted people who would listen and be willing to open doors for others.

When we spend too much time looking at our deficiencies, we lose sight of what is still possible. Alexander Graham Bell said, "When one door closes another door opens; but we so often look so long and so regretfully upon the closed door, that we do not see the ones which open for us."

God opens doors for you every day, and He invites you to discover all that is still possible for you. Look to Him for some new direction.

Lord, thank You for continuing to open new doors for me. Help me to see the opportunities you offer with renewed energy and focus. I pray I will embrace those things that make my life more meaningful and productive. Amen.

79

The Possibility Gene

John will be a great man for the Lord. He will never drink wine or
beer, and even from birth, he will be filled with the Holy Spirit.

LUKE 1:15 NCV

We give genetics a lot of credit or blame for who we are and what we're able to do. We appreciate inheriting Dad's youthful looks or Mom's incredible skill at mathematics. We love having sparkling eyes and a delicate nose. So what would we do if we had a possibility gene, something built right into our DNA that gave us a sense of eternal optimism and hope for the future?

It turns out we do! We have a heavenly Father, and we've inherited amazing things from Him. The better we know Him, the more we grow up to be like Him. Faith was built into our DNA the day we accepted Jesus into our lives. God gave us a bit of Himself so that we connect easily to Him. We are filled with His Spirit, and that Spirit grants us rights and privileges inherited directly from our Father.

Your earthly parents helped you become self-sufficient and capable of managing life. They provided for your primary needs, but their DNA is only part of your story. God wants even more for you.

If all things are possible with God, then the Holy Spirit is your possibility gene. He's the catalyst for new ideas and the nudge when an opportunity presents itself. He's the still, small voice cheering you on to begin anew. He's the extraordinary parent who sees all you can be and loves you into becoming all you were meant to be.

Your possibility gene flares up when you feel defeated or discouraged. It cycles back around when you need some time just to get your bearings. When you became a child of God, your DNA changed to make room in your heart, enlarging its potential to take in more of what God wanted for you. If you're not sure what to do now, then sit back and pray. Ask the Holy Spirit to show you what would please Him. He enjoys a good parent/child chat that helps you see what is still possible.

Lord God, You are my heavenly Father, and though You have a lot of children, I know that You don't have another one quite like me. Help me to make You proud as I consider my direction in life. Thank You for the gift of Your Holy Spirit to guide me and shape my heart. Amen.

80

Never Say Never!

My God will use his wonderful riches in Christ
Jesus to give you everything you need.
PHILIPPIANS 4:19 NCV

o you have a bucket list? Do you list things you would love to do, and even some you will never do? Your "never" list might include things like bungee jumping over Niagara Falls or learning to bull fight—both sound choices. Maybe your "hopeful" bucket list includes learning a new language or visiting the pyramids in Egypt. This list is a picture of your optimism and your faith.

Your bucket list reminds you of things that seem out of reach but may be possible if you create a plan to achieve them. They are attainable goals that need a bit of work. You hold them up as a possibility.

What about creating goals for your bucket list that require discipline and study, even more than time and money? Maybe you want to run a 5K when you're sixty-five and finish in the top 10 percent. If you have never entered a race before, this may seem far-fetched,; but with practice and discipline, it is achievable.

What about setting goals where you risk failure? Perhaps you'd like to try out for community theater, but you are nervous because you haven't acted in years. If you don't try out, you never get a part in the play. Is it still possible for you to get out of your own way and bring this goal to fruition?

Another side of your bucket list could be spiritual. Maybe you could preach a sermon or sing in the choir? Maybe you can receive gifts of the Holy Spirit? Seek God's direction for ways you could serve Him. Begin somewhere; that beginning might lead to sweet fulfillment.

You can create a bucket list. However, if you think what you want will never be possible, you have written the script already. You stand in the way of all God wants for you. It's time to stop the noises in your head and step up. Give your heart's desires to God and never say never again!

Lord God, I suspect I have shut the door on more than a few opportunities simply because I was afraid. I've had a self-fulfilling attitude that assumed I could never do it. Help me to build a new bucket list, full of plans to cultivate a deeper faith in You. Amen.

81

Yes, You Can!

But Jesus was matter-of-fact: "Yes—and if you embrace this
kingdom life and don't doubt God, you'll not only do minor feats
like I did to the fig tree, but also triumph over huge obstacles."

MATTHEW 21:21 MSG

oubt is not a particularly charming player in the game of
life. It walks along with fear and causes everyone to step
back as it passes by. It takes the most beautiful idea and strikes a
hole in it, wrenching possibility from its hand. It's a dark shadow
that only comes close enough to the light to cause dismay.

In this example, Jesus spoke to His disciples about the fig
tree that He caused to wither and die. The fig tree had not pro-
duced any fruit, only leaves, and since Jesus and His followers
were hungry, Jesus expressed His disappointment by telling the
tree it would never produce fruit again. To the amazement of His
disciples, the tree withered up. The disciples wondered how it
was possible for Jesus to simply speak to the tree and cause that
outcome.

The answer in part is that Jesus knew who He was. He knew
what was possible. He knew how powerful the spoken word was

because He was with God at the very beginning, when God spoke all of creation into existence. Jesus had no doubt about the effect His words would have on the tree.

What would it take for you to speak without doubt, expecting every word to be fulfilled? What would it take for you to believe that God has already designed your next possibility and He is walking just ahead of you to pave the way?

If you're hungry for new direction, go to God and seek His confirmation of those things you believe you are meant to do. After that, move forward with confidence, knowing you are not alone and you are meant to succeed. God wants to hear you say out loud, "Yes! I can do it!"

When you have confidence, God creates opportunities and circumstances to propel you toward your goal. There will be no time for doubt. In fact, doubt will wither up and blow away.

Lord, I have often tried to do new things with half a heart. Please wash away my fears and doubts so that I simply believe the encouragement and possibility you have spoken into my heart. I praise You and thank You. Amen.

82

Weary of Waiting

*Meanwhile, the moment we get tired in the waiting, God's Spirit
is right alongside helping us along. If we don't know how or what
to pray, it doesn't matter. He does our praying in and for us,
making prayer out of our wordless sighs, our aching groans.*
ROMANS 8:26 MSG

You believe you are ready to embark on some whole new
waters, but you hesitate. You've been petitioning God spe-
cifically in prayer, but you wonder if you've failed to know His
will and are perhaps praying the wrong prayer. You put your toe
in the water and pull it out again. Maybe next time. Maybe you'll
simply wait a little longer. But you are tired of waiting.

Take heart. Your inability to know God's will is met by His
Spirit, who Himself expresses to God the desires of your heart
that perfectly match the will of God. When you do not know
what to pray for—yes, even when you pray for things that are not
best for you—you need not despair, for you can depend on the
Spirit's ministry of perfect intercession on your behalf.

So if you are tired of waiting in any area of your life, or even
if you're not sure what you're waiting for, then be encouraged

to keep praying. If you're not sure whether you can manage the winds of change, then pray some more. If you're wondering how to express your concerns to God, stop and be silent before Him. He already knows the things that are on your mind, so simply give Him thanks and praise because the Holy Spirit has prayed for you.

Answers to your prayers are still possible. Release the rope that keeps your boat tied to the dock. Set your course and anticipate the balmy breezes. Trust that God is with you wherever you go and that He believes in all that you want to accomplish in His will. The waiting is over. Believe that all things are possible with God. *Bon voyage!*

Lord God, I believe You want me to stop waiting and start doing something. I pray You will encourage me to trust that through the Holy Spirit You hear my prayer and want me to keep taking more steps in faith, believing I have found Your direction for my life. Thank You for guiding my little vessel once again. Amen.

83

Can You Believe That?

So they asked him, "What sign then will you give that
we may see it and believe you? What will you do?"
JOHN 6:30

ost of us say we believe God can do anything. We say that because we recognize if God is God, then He is truly in control. That's a great big-picture thought. Now make it specific to you. Can God do anything *for you*? Can He create new possibilities *for you*?

You may have no trouble saying God can do anything, but when it comes to shaping your life and fixing the messes you find yourself in, well, that feels different. After all, God has more important matters on His plate. You may not imagine you're worthy of God taking time to step in to help.

So what do we do? We ask for signs. We ask for tangible evidence that God is with us.

Being gracious, God honors our prayers and offers us opportunities to discover He is near. He's been creating that evidence ever since the first rainbow appeared. Some wonder whether God only did signs and wonders for the ancients or if He still does them today. Martyn Lloyd-Jones said, "It is perfectly clear that in the New Testament times, the gospel was authenticated in this way, by signs, wonders, and miracles of various characters and descriptions. . . . Was it only to be true of the early church? . . . The Scriptures never anywhere say that these things were only temporary—never! There is no such statement anywhere."

The God of the possible is still interested in helping you anytime and anywhere. He wants you to believe in Him with your whole heart, surrendering all you are and putting your life in His hands. When you do, He is ready to help you with His amazing grace and power. He will offer you ways to recognize His presence. All you have to do is believe!

Lord God, I do believe You can do anything, but I admit I often stand aside from that belief when it comes to my own needs. Thank You for providing me with a real sense of Your presence any time I surrender my heart to You. I praise You and thank You, Lord, for the wondrous gift of Your redeeming grace. Amen.

84

Possibility Leaves a Trail

In all your ways submit to him, and he will make your paths straight.

PROVERBS 3:6

D o you ever get so immersed in your work or in your parenting, or even in your church duties, that you feel dizzy just thinking about what must be accomplished? When you get overwhelmed, you may find you're not just wandering away from a designated path but that you struggle to find your way back again.

We can walk crooked pathways without realizing how we got there. Our ancestor Jacob wrestled with God all night long and wouldn't give up until he won. He finally looked up and saw the heavens open and a ladder emerge with angels going up and down. Jacob knew God was with him, and He had great plans for him. You can read about his experience in Genesis 28:10–19 in your favorite translation.

Unfortunately, we wrestle with life more often than we wrestle with God. We work hard and we struggle. Each one of our concerns—bills, our health, family relationships, or work challenges—can sway us from the path, leaving a trail of dissolution and sadness. Nobody wins. When our focus is on things that cause us to worry, we fall behind. We become numb to God's presence. Every possibility we thought we had dries up and blows away.

What can we do? We can stop wrestling with life's challenges and turn our focus toward things that bring hope. We can seek the path God wants for us and leave a trail for those who come behind. We can remind ourselves to stay connected to our Redeemer.

If you pay attention, you'll discover more of God's Spirit leading you forward. You'll climb the ladder of success . . . in the sense that you will be looking up, intentionally searching for God's face.

When you walk with God, amazing things happen. You are carving out a path for those who come behind you because they want to know what you know. They want to follow you to discover more about how they, too, can walk with God. May God bless you and keep you on the straight path to glory.

Lord, help me walk with You each day and not get ahead of You. Remind me to look up so that I may see You working on my behalf. I pray for the guiding light of Your Spirit as I go into this new day. Amen.

85

It's Just Not Possible!

*"I am the LORD, the God of every person on the
earth. Nothing is impossible for me."*

JEREMIAH 32:27 NCV

Remember the woman who came up behind Jesus and believed if she could just touch His garment, she would be healed? Well, she did, and Jesus rewarded her faith. The woman was ill for twelve years. She was powerless to do anything about her ailment. She may have thought, *It's just not possible for me to be healed.* However, her faith encouraged her to believe that, if she could just follow Jesus, she might yet be healed.

God asks the same of us. Will we trust and follow Him, moving toward the possibilities only He can offer? He knows we get discouraged. He knows we suffer things that are hard to bear, but He says, "Don't give up. Don't worry because all things are possible for Me!"

Michael Jordan was assigned to the junior varsity team in high school. He learned that when you fail, you have to try again and take another shot. Though Winston Churchill failed the sixth grade, he would later become prime minister of Great

Britain and win the Nobel Prize in Literature. Not bad for a guy who couldn't make it through grade school.

The inventor who lights up your life, Thomas Edison, was considered "too stupid to learn anything" by his grade-school teachers. He lost jobs because he appeared to be a daydreamer, and finally after trying a thousand times, managed to create a light bulb. He never said, "It's just not possible!"

As you move forward in your life, refrain from using a word like *impossible*. Refuse to set limits on yourself. Instead, surrender everything you are to the One who loves you beyond measure and allow Him to shape you into becoming the best you possible.

Lord of the Possible, help me to leave negative thinking, discouraging words, and doubt behind, and to pick up the banner of trust, hope, and faith. Help me to believe with my whole heart in those things that are still possible for me. Amen.

86

Hope on Fire

I pray that your hearts will be flooded with light so that you can
understand the confident hope he has given to those he called—
his holy people who are his rich and glorious inheritance.

EPHESIANS 1:18 NLT

Frank C. Laubach, missionary and founder of the Laubach
Way to Reading, wanted to bring hope and peace to others
by helping people learn to read. He gave speeches around the
world about compassion and hope. He said, "When compassion
for the common man was born on Christmas Day, with it was
born new hope among the multitudes. They feel a great, ever-
rising determination to lift themselves and their children out of
hunger and disease and misery, up to a higher level. Jesus started
a fire upon the earth, and it is burning hot today, the fire of a new
hope in the hearts of the hungry multitudes."

Hope and possibility both light a fire in our hearts to answer
the call of God to light up the world. Those holy ideals burn
within us so that we never give up on making the effort to be His
people. We don't have to travel the world as missionaries, but
we can be ambassadors of God's love and kindness in our own

neighborhoods. Ambassadors speak a word of hope and create an atmosphere of possibility. God plants seeds of hope in our hearts to keep the eternal flame lit. He knows what we need, and He knows that without His help, we can do nothing.

You act as His ambassador when you pray from a heart of forgiveness and kindness. You offer the fire of possibility by being gracious and optimistic. You make a difference, and that difference brings possibility. You are blessed to be a blessing and to make opportunities come alive for those around you.

No matter what is going on for you today, be the fire that lights up possibilities in the hearts and minds of others. When you do, possibilities light up for you as well. God will bless your efforts over and over again.

Lord God, You have blessed me in ways too numerous to count. You light the way for me when I get back on the path, causing my little candle to shine brightly. Father, help me believe in every possibility You share with me so I can pass on the flame of Your love to those around me. Amen.

87

Mission: Impossible

*But we ought always to thank God for you, brothers and sisters loved
by the Lord, because God chose you as firstfruits to be saved through
the sanctifying work of the Spirit and through belief in the truth.*

2 THESSALONIANS 2:13

If you've ever watched one of the *Mission: Impossible* films,
you've seen Ethan Hunt lead his team, the IMF, or Impossible
Missions Force, through one death-defying act after another.
These are some of the best "impossible scenes" that movie mak-
ers can imagine. As soon as Ethan's IMF team is called in, he
knows the job ahead can't be done by just anybody. It has to be
done by him! Since the first film released, we've been witnesses to
the fantastic efforts of this team on mission after mission. They
do their job so well we almost forget they are mere human beings.

In the film world, impossible missions somehow are always
pulled off. We might envy that because in the real world even
everyday missions can feel impossible. As a believer, you have a
mission that no one else can accomplish quite the way you can.
God equipped you with unique talents to pull the job off. You
may not be called to stop a nuclear explosion, but your mission

is just as important. Your mission is to hold up the light so others can find their way to God. The adversary in your mission is more threatening than anything Ethan Hunt will ever face.

You may wonder if anything makes a difference in a world poised for destruction. If it's all up to you, it is a mission: impossible. Fortunately, it's not all in your hands. God brings people into your life who help with the work you do, and He watches over everything. With Him, everything about your mission is possible.

If you wonder what might still be possible, look at how God has equipped you to do a new job. God's question is, "Will you go and get the job done?" Ethan Hunt's team may disavow his actions if he's caught, but you can be sure your team will be right there with you. Nothing about your call and your important message will self-destruct in five seconds. It's the work of eternity.

God, I feel secure in Your strong hands, knowing You will help me as I do my work. I praise You for being the greatest force in this universe. Help me to take on my mission with love. I believe in what is still possible. Amen.

88

Nobody Quite Like You

I praise you because I am fearfully and wonderfully made;
your works are wonderful, I know that full well.

PSALM 139:14

You are designed as a one-of-a-kind, no-blueprint-necessary kind of person. You stand up for what you believe, you rise to the occasion to lend a helping hand, and you have a smile that competes with the sun on a cloudy day. There's simply no one quite like you.

In case you're wondering, that's how God feels about you as well. He sees your heart and knows you like no one else can. He sees you and wants you to trust that everything about you matters.

As you've traveled through life, you've learned what's important to you. You've discovered great relationships, how they work, and how they sometimes fall apart. You've learned from poor choices, seeking God's grace and forgiveness.

You see God's hand in the details of your life, in every choice you've made. As you stand in the present, and when you choose to look up, you see Him leaning in to hear your prayers and doing all He can to hold you up. With that kind of experience, it makes sense that God is planning even more for you, preparing to reveal what's next for you. He is creating options for you to enjoy those things that are still possible.

God never gets weary of watching over you. He doesn't send a committee to make decisions about you, and He doesn't rely on hearsay or anybody else's opinion. He doesn't have to. He simply knows there is only one you and He designed you perfectly. It is His good pleasure to share every possible joy with you in the days ahead.

Give God credit for every good thing you have, and seek His face for all that is still possible in your future. He's always near you. Just look up!

Lord, I know You are the great Designer, the One who blessed me with a loving spirit, a kind heart, and certain talents and skills. I am grateful for each of those things. Help me to start with You with every choice I make so I might please You and grow in Your grace and mercy. Amen.

89

Inner Boundaries and Outer Limits

*Then the devil led Jesus to . . . a high place of the
Temple. He said to Jesus, "If you are the Son of God,
jump down. It is written in the Scriptures: 'He has put
his angels in charge of you to watch over you.'"*

LUKE 4:9–10 NCV

We all know about temptation. It seeks you out when things
aren't going as they should. It offers solutions that are
temporary at best and harmful at worst. It yanks your chain to see
where you've set your inner boundaries. It doesn't care if you're
hurting or fearful. It doesn't look to see if the thing that tempts
you will make your life even more uncomfortable. It simply serves
to distract you from the one thing that is important—your faith
and your worship of God.

When Jesus was tempted by Satan in the desert, He was hungry and tired and had been through things that would weaken
the spirit of anyone, even the Son of God. Satan knew if he could
distract Jesus, he could whittle away at His faith and His future
possibility. The beauty of this passage is that it helps us in our
temptation as well. If we resist temptation and set limits to stay

within God's grasp, we're better off. Faith, which sets our boundaries, helps us navigate life and direct our efforts toward future possibilities.

God sees you in the midst of your trials and understands the reasons for the things that tempt you. Stop! Look up! Remember your life is more valuable to Him than anything. He provided you with an escape from temptation because He wants you to resist the devil. "Resist the devil, and he will flee from you" (James 4:7). When you feel that all your possibilities have drained away and you're tempted to take an action that will not serve you well, just stop!

Set your outer boundaries, and your inner faith will sustain you. God forgives the mistakes of yesterday. Try once more to resist temptations that do not serve you, and reach out to God, the only One who can help you find new hope and direction.

Lord God, I am often tempted to take the path that takes me nowhere. Help me to remember who I am in You so I can resist the devil and run as far and fast from him as possible. Remind me to surrender only to You, the Creator of all my hope and possibility. Amen.

90

Of Sense and Possibility

*They make the uneducated wise and give knowledge
and sense to the young. Wise people can also listen and
learn; even they can find good advice in these words.*

PROVERBS 1:4–5 NCV

o you remember any of those "momisms" you heard growing up? Maybe your mom said you had to eat your broccoli because poor children were starving and would love to have your vegetables, or that she had eyes in the back of her head and always knew what you were doing. No matter what your mom had to say, you learned to listen, and when you grew up, you found yourself saying some of those same things. You know, things like, "Close the door! Did you grow up in a barn?"

We need adages that keep us grounded and scriptures that give us strength at just the right moment. We need those proverbs that Solomon and others wrote to help us live honestly and purposefully. Perhaps you couldn't make sense of all those things your mom said as a child, but with time you recognized that each tender morsel of thought actually provided you with a bit more possibility.

Sometimes in our walk of faith, things don't make sense to us. We can't understand how we managed to make a mess of things or how we were blindsided by something important. We wonder if we even have any common sense at all.

Common sense doesn't seem so common after all. You may have noticed that in your own life. What makes sense to you as a person of faith? Trial and error? Or listening to the sweet voice of God?

All that is possible for you may be wrapped in some form of common sense or the sayings of those you admire. Chances are that what makes sense to God may not be exactly what you expected. What makes sense to God is that He will always lead the way into every possibility.

Lord of heaven and earth, I am not always sure what makes sense to those around me. Thank You for the encouraging things my mother once said to remind me to keep trying and not give up. Thank You for the scriptures that encourage my walk with You. Amen.

91

A Hallmark Moment

The LORD's Spirit spoke through me, and his word was on my tongue.
2 SAMUEL 23:2 NCV

When you care enough to send the very best" is the Hallmark slogan of excellence. It's a phrase you know so well it can roll off the tip of your tongue. When Joyce Clyde Hall began selling his greeting cards from shoeboxes back in the early 1900s, he probably never imagined how it would grow. His company has been impacting the lives of others for more than one hundred years because Hall went after every possibility he could find.

Whether you want to start a business or try something you've never tried before, you need to be bold. Opportunity comes and goes, and the only ones who make things happen are those who step up and try and try again. Possibility is fickle, so you have to do more than flirt with it if you hope to embrace all that it has to offer.

Because of J. C. Hall's vision, we ascribe picturesque, idyllic events in our lives as "Hallmark" moments. We can use a greeting card to express joy, encouragement, or meaningful moments in our lives. We can celebrate our victories, and others will share our stories.

When a word is important, we hold it close, sometimes on the tips of our tongues. We want to remember its power and purpose. We should hold our vision for possibility close to the heart, offer it to God, and then go after it. That's why words of wisdom or bits of Scripture remain in our hearts and minds. We protect them and work with them to make them ours. As the owner of your possibilities, consider what you will do to achieve your goals and find your purpose.

J. C. Hall, quoting Theodore Roosevelt, said that when we get to the end of our rope, we have to tie a knot and hang on. It's good advice for any of us who might be looking to celebrate a Hallmark moment. You can do it! God's got you covered.

Lord, thank You for giving me this idea, this vision, this hope to be fulfilled. Help me to be willing to go after it, staying faithful to Your call. I pray that You will help me to discover all that is still possible today. Amen.

92

It's your Turn!

"So those who are last now will be first then,
and those who are first will be last."
MATTHEW 20:16 NLT

You've experienced the twists and turns of life. You head
in one direction, thinking you know exactly where you're
bound. But then the proverbial road washes out, leaving you
wondering where to go next. You start to back up and cruise
along just fine for a while, then you are stopped cold once again.
You grow weary of having to change gears to make life work out.
You wonder if anything you want in life is still possible!

No one can tell you that all your dreams will come true or
that you're about to catch that one lucky break. No one, that is,
but God. With billions of people on the planet, you might reason
that God can't be overly concerned with your dreams. He can't
just call your name and tell you that it's your turn. Or can He?

It is a matter of timing and faith. D. L. Moody said, "Faith
takes God without any ifs. If God says anything, faith says, 'I
believe it;' and faith says, 'Amen' to it." Faith moves you past
stuck places, past wrong turns and roadblocks. Faith says, "It's

your turn!" If you believe it and can say "Amen" to it, then God is speaking to your heart and asking you to keep moving forward. Faith is the key component to all possibility. Without it, we are lost!

It's important to have faith in your dreams, but it's even more important to have faith in God. With God's help, amazing things can happen. Without His help, you may find yourself switching gears over and over again. When it's your turn to achieve your dreams, He will be with you the whole way, and nothing will be able to stop you. Let your prayer be willing to wait for God's timing and God's direction. It's the perfect way to find all that is still possible. Your turn is coming!

Lord God, I am heavy-footed on the gas pedal of my life sometimes. I know I peel out and get ahead of You, losing my way in the process. Help me to wait my turn and seek Your direction in all I do. Help me embrace Your perfect timing. Amen.

93

Those Someday Dreams

When Jesus came to Simon Peter, Peter said to him, "Lord,
are you going to wash my feet?" Jesus replied, "You don't
understand now what I am doing, but someday you will."

JOHN 13:6–7 NLT

ou may remember being a confused kid and question-
ing your parents about something that was going on.
They probably told you that you would understand "someday."
Someday seems to be a great place to hang our hats even though
we seldom have a sense of when it will arrive.

No doubt Jesus' followers remembered His words as they
moved on without Him in the days after His resurrection. They
realized He was giving them a picture of what it means to surrender the ego and to serve Him with a fully committed heart.
They discovered that "someday" was a lot closer than they had
once thought.

Most of us have things we're intent on doing someday. We
think we'll travel somewhere wonderful, or buy an RV, or perhaps
learn a new language. We actually leave a lot of things out there
to be accomplished . . . someday.

What progress are you making on your someday list? Has anything moved off to become a "today" thing? Someday is just beyond our reach, outside of our grasp. C. S. Lewis wrote, "The next moment is as much beyond our grasp, and as much in God's care, as that a hundred years away. Care for the next minute is just as foolish as care for a day in the next thousand years. In neither can we do anything; in both God is doing everything."

How will you awaken your "someday" dreams? Perhaps the best answer is to grasp the present and give God the opportunity to hold open the doors to what He intends for you. Stay close to the One who holds your dreams.

Lord of All, I don't know what tomorrow will bring or when someday will come, but I am willing to leave any future possibilities in Your hand. I seek Your face for each thing I do. I pray to be all that I can be for You today, and I leave "someday" in Your hands. Amen.

94

Impossible!

God did this so that, by two unchangeable things in which
it is impossible for God to lie, we who have fled to take hold
of the hope set before us may be greatly encouraged.

HEBREWS 6:18

Most of us would say we do our best not to tell a lie. However, on closer review, we might realize that actually saying we don't lie is a lie in itself. The problem is that we excuse ourselves when we tell white lies or when we exaggerate the details of our story to make it sound more significant.

We get away with those things because we don't consider them to be lies, just ways to spare the feelings of others. Okay, but what about the lies we tell ourselves? What about the lies rooted in past experience? The idea that "I couldn't do it then, so I probably can't do it now" is damaging to our dreams.

In fact, the lies we tell ourselves may be the most harmful of all. They become part of our story line, repeated until we can't dismiss them. That old liar, Satan, reminds us over and again of our failings and our sinfulness, doing his best to keep us insecure in our relationship with God. When we buy into his lies, we step back from God, uncertain as to whether He really loves us or cares about the things that matter to us.

The writer of Hebrews says God can't lie. God is love. God is truth. God is only good and therefore He can't lie. When God says "I love you," He means it. He means it so much He not only redeems you and brings you hope, but He goes wherever you are, to the depths of the ocean if need be, bringing you up from the shadowy waters into the light of His saving grace and love.

God wants you to tell the truth, not just to Him or to others but to yourself as well. In truth you will discover your real calling, your genuine possibilities. Truth sets you free to be more than you ever imagined.

Lord of All Truth, I tell myself lies that keep me from moving forward. I am shattered by the voices in my head that remind me of my failures, and I get stuck there. Help me to turn to You so I can discover all that is still possible in Your sight. Amen.

95

Rock, Paper, Scissors

*"The rain came down, the streams rose, and the winds
blew and beat against that house; yet it did not fall,
because it had its foundation on the rock."*

MATTHEW 7:25

Remember playing a game called Rock, Paper, Scissors to help pass the time? It's an interesting game that originates from the ancient Chinese. Starting in the 1920s, parents in the United States used it as a game to help kids settle squabbles. All in all, it was a good thing!

In our analogy we'll call the rock your foundation, your faith in Christ. In the child's game, the rock only beats the scissors; in our game, the Rock beats everything. Your faith will get you where you want to go because it is the cornerstone of your life. Winds may blow and storms may flood the landscape, but nothing will remove the Rock of your salvation.

Scissors beats paper when you play the child's game. If your paper is a list of your dreams and possibilities, then let scissors represent your prayers that help you cut down your options.

Some of your original dreams will fall away as you take them to God in prayer.

Admittedly, the analogy isn't perfect, but perhaps the connection to the childhood game will remind you of what's true as you pursue your dreams. The list on your paper is worthy of prayer. The scissors of prayer are great tools to snip out weak ideas, and the rock of God's steadfast and faithful love will always be present. When you put all your hopes and plans in God's hand, you can be sure He will take it from there. In fact, you can bet on it! The Rock wins every time!

Lord, I don't always know the good choices to make, so I place all my dreams and ideas into Your hands, asking You to guide me to do the right thing. Thank You for your steadfast faithfulness and for being the Rock of my salvation. Amen.

96

Change Is in the Air!

Every good and perfect gift is from above, coming
down from the Father of the heavenly lights, who
does not change like shifting shadows.
JAMES 1:17

When change is in the air, we either welcome it or try to avoid it altogether. We look to the future, cling tightly to the past, and somehow forget to live in the current moment. All the while, we know that change is coming our way.

Sometimes we are so resistant to change we've made a new opportunity virtually impossible. We convince ourselves that our hopes and dreams are too far-fetched to pursue. We settle into daily routines that neither challenge nor fulfill us.

We need to change, but we don't know how to go about it. God wants us to change for the better so we can truly serve Him with wholehearted love. Change is good, but it takes courage.

The good news is that God never changes. He's the same yesterday, today, and forever, and He knows we need Him to remain constant. We need to know that He is our refuge no matter how far we wander or how long it takes us to turn around.

Knowing we have an all-powerful God frees us to put our toes in the waters of change. We can try new things, make mistakes, and change our minds, and it will all be good. We get to know the truth of who we are and who God wants us to be.

Possibilities may bring significant change into your life. They may bring new perspectives. You can hold on to the Rock of your soul, the One who seeks even now to inspire your dreams, knowing He invites you to change and get to know Him better than you do now. Change is in the air! It's not a matter of change for the sake of change but change for the sake of all God meant for you. Your day is loaded with possibilities!

Lord of Steadfast Love, I do not always like change. Help me, Lord, to be more open to those changes that will keep me in tune to Your desires for my life. Inspire me to seek future possibilities, knowing I can trust You to always be there for me. Amen.

97

At the Heart of Success

"Always remember what is written in the Book of the Teachings.
Study it day and night to be sure to obey everything that is written
there. If you do this, you will be wise and successful in everything."

JOSHUA 1:8 NCV

You're successful! However you define success, you have greatly succeeded at many things in your life. In some ways, you've even exceeded your own expectations. It's amazing! As you contemplate what's still possible for you, you may not feel an urgent need to go exploring. You may feel quite satisfied with the way things are.

Success is a layered pursuit. It is built on a foundation and comes together with hard work and persistence. It's been said that every great achievement was once considered impossible. You've faced the impossible before. You've looked at it squarely and watched as it came into focus in ways that brought you closer to meeting your goals. You've been at the top in one way or another.

Winston Churchill said that success is never final. When you reach a mountaintop in one area, you see the view of many other mountaintops yet to climb. The good news is you are not trying to achieve more just for the sake of achievement. You are trying to become everything God designed you to be.

You've got new levels of success and new possibilities still waiting for you. If you're pretty sure there's more you can do, then step out in faith, reach up in joy, and seek God's face. He will ensure your success because He knows you've put your heart into it. May God bless you with great favor and success beyond measure.

Lord God, You've enriched my life, broadened my reach in the work I do, and prospered me. I pray to keep my heart aligned with Yours and to do all I can to grow in love and compassion toward others. Thank You for your continual guidance and love. I look forward to all that You will do through me. Amen.

98

The Blue Book of Possibility

*Jesus performed many other signs in the presence of
his disciples, which are not recorded in this book.*
JOHN 20:30

If you're thinking of trading in your car, you might go to a resource known as the Kelley Blue Book to get an idea of its value. Based on the mileage, the condition of the car, the make and model, and so on, you can get an idea of its worth. It's become a pretty reliable tool, and many car dealers use it as a ready reference.

We might say God has a "blue book" too. It's called the Book of Life, and He already has your name in it. Everyone whose name is recorded there will get the green light from those who usher people through the gates of heaven because your value has already been determined.

Jesus is the Source for all of our possibilities. He has placed an incredible value on us, and we cannot comprehend it. The interesting thing is that our value does not decline with having a few miles or a few scraped fenders on us. We've still got top value in His book.

The best thing we can do is to strive to please Him throughout our lifetime. We can chart a new course, design a new plan, and go after those things we neglected somewhere else along the way. We can become more of what He wants simply because He is cheering us on and helping to strengthen our souls. If we need a complete overhaul, as long as we've got the right inner workings, He can do that too. In fact, there's nothing about us He can't fix and make shiny and whole again.

Improvements are still possible. All you have to do is get out of the driver's seat and let God in. It's going to be a great day to cruise along with the One who loves you and values you.

Lord, thank You for always valuing me. Help me to do what I can to stay closely connected to Your Spirit so I can shine on the open road or even just parked in my driveway. I know there's a lot more that I can do, and I am ready any time to get tuned up so that I am at my best for You. Amen.

99

The Possibility Challenge

Everyone who competes in the games goes into strict training. They do it to get a crown that will not last, but we do it to get a crown that will last forever.

1 CORINTHIANS 9:25

*Y*ou are always in training. You may not go out to lift weights every day or sit in a classroom building your academic skills, but God issued a challenge to you when you were born, and you are still trying to meet it. What was the challenge?

You have been given an opportunity. You have gifts and talents and abilities that no one else has in quite the same way. You have unique insights and perspectives and hopes and dreams. You have a heart that is continually being developed and nourished. It is stretched and sometimes broken. It is healed and replenished because it is in a process of continual training and softening. God works best with soft hearts.

You've been gearing up, practicing, and running the race, and you're fully equipped to go the distance. Now God is asking you to consider this: *What is still possible for me? What can I do that will make a difference to those around me, to my family and friends, and most of all in my service to God?*

That's the possibility challenge. You have nothing to fear. You have everything you need to go forward, and the One who makes all things possible for you goes before you. Imagine, this is your big moment, the blue-ribbon chance to give God your best. Nothing can stop you now!

Lord God, You know me so well. You have trusted me to handle some tough situations in my life and helped me to press on and move forward. You have given me courage when I felt weak and prompted me to try again when things did not work out as I expected. Give me a soft heart and inspire my direction so I can be all You have dreamed I would be. I accept the challenge and I'm glad to be on Your team. Amen.

100

It's Still Possible!

Jesus looked at them and said, "With man this is
impossible, but with God all things are possible."
MATTHEW 19:26

Only you can define what "it" is—that thing that is still possible for you. It can be many things, of course. You might want it to be the fulfillment of a long-held dream like buying a new home or moving to another part of the country. You may want to find success in your profession, finally getting that long overdue promotion or being acknowledged by your peers in a generous way.

Sometimes that thing you want, the "it," is not for you but for someone else. You want your child to get off drugs and become whole and healthy. You want your friend to get counseling to overcome depression. Your prayers and your hopes are for the good of those around you.

Your possibility dream may be one you haven't clearly defined, though your restless spirit says it's there. If you have given up on dreams, you may not recognize God is with you, seeking to help you find your true North.

Forgiveness is still possible! Love is stronger than all other issues, even those that have damaged your pride or injured your spirit. Remember how often God has forgiven you and continued to love you and show up for the things that matter most to you.

A deeper relationship with God is still possible. Tell Him you want your relationship with Him to shine with infinite possibility despite your past behaviors and your long list of sins. Put all those things at God's feet and He will show you all that is yet to be. In God's hands, you have endless possibilities. All you need to do is let Him know you believe that with His help, things you never imagined could be are possible.

Wash away the cares of yesterday and give yourself permission to open a new door. Let God define "it" for you and show you the way to all that is still possible!

Lord God, thank You for helping me to draw closer to You, trusting Your direction and believing in all that You want for me. Guide me in ways that will bring me peace of mind and heart and allow me to do those things that please You. Thank You for being the God of All That Is Still Possible! Amen.